W9-CMT-151

Birds of Wisconsin

Field Guide
Second Edition

by Stan Tekiela

Adventure Publications, Inc.
Cambridge, Minnesota

To my wife Katherine and daughter Abigail with all my love

Acknowledgments

Special thanks to the National Wildlife Refuge System, which stewards the land that is critical to many bird species.

Edited by Sandy Livoti

Cover, book and CD design and illustrations by Jonathan Norberg

Range maps produced by Anthony Hertzel

Photo credits by photographer and page number:
Cover photo: American Robin by Bill Marchel
Brian M. Collins: 211, 231 **Dudley Edmondson**: 17 (perching), 19 (soaring), 67, 79, 83, 91 (female), 127 (both), 141 (soaring), 161 (both), 183, 185, 189 (male), 197 (perching, soaring), 201 (breeding), 239 (in flight), 241 (breeding), 251 (winter male), 253 (male), 255 (male), 261 **Bill Marchel**: 63 (male), 93 (white-striped), 97, 101 (adult), 109, 121, 141 (perching), 209 (both), 217 (male), 223, 237 (male), 247 (in flight) **Maslowski Wildlife Productions**: 23 (female), 69 (soaring), 99, 167, 229, 257, 259 **Steve Mortensen**: 29 (male), 41 (both), 51, 55, 89 (both) **Warren Nelson**: 29 (female), 129 (female), 255 (female) **John Pennoyer**: 75 **Johann Schumacher/CLO***: 63 (female) **Brian E. Small**: 37, 85, 111 (winter), 135, 201 (winter, juvenile), 225 (yellow male), 241 (winter) **Ben Sosniecki**: 101 (juvenile) **Stan Tekiela**: 1, 3, 5 (both), 7, 9, 11, 13, 15, 17 (in flight), 19 (perching), 21 (all), 23 (male), 25 (both), 27, 31 (both), 33, 35 (both), 39, 43, 45 (both), 47 (both), 49 (all), 53, 57 (both), 59 (both), 61, 65, 69 (perching), 71, 73 (both), 77, 81, 87, 91 (male), 93 (tan-striped), 95 (both), 103 (adult, 1 year old), 105, 107, 111 (breeding), 113 (female, juvenile), 115, 117 (all), 119, 123, 125, 129 (male), 131, 133 (both), 137, 139 (both), 143 (both), 145, 147, 149, 151, 153, 155, 157 (both), 159 (perching male, soaring male and female), 163, 165 (all), 169 (both), 171 (both), 173 (all), 175, 177, 179, 181, 187, 189 (female), 191 (both), 193, 195, 197 (juvenile), 201 (in flight), 203 (both), 205 (all), 207 (both), 213, 215, 217 (in flight), 219, 221, 225 (male), 227, 233 (male), 235, 237 (in flight), 239 (perching), 241 (juvenile), 243 (all), 245 (both), 247 (swimming, juvenile), 249, 251 (male, female), 263 (all), 265 **Brian K. Wheeler**: 159 (perching female), 199 (all) **Jim Zipp**: 103 (Bohemian), 253 (female)
*Cornell Laboratory of Ornithology

To the best of the publisher's knowledge, all photos were of live birds.

10 9 8
Second Edition 2004
Copyright 1999 by Stan Tekiela
Published by Adventure Publications, Inc.
820 Cleveland Street South
Cambridge, MN 55008
1-800-678-7006
www.adventurepublications.net
All rights reserved
Printed in China
ISBN: 978-1-59193-040-2

TABLE OF CONTENTS

Introduction

Sample Page

The Birds

Helpful Resources

Checklist/Index by Species

About the Author

WHY WATCH BIRDS IN WISCONSIN?

Millions of people have discovered bird feeding. It's a simple and enjoyable way to bring the beauty of birds closer to your home. Watching birds at your feeder and listening to them often leads to a lifetime pursuit of bird identification. The *Birds of Wisconsin Field Guide* is for those who want to identify the common birds of Wisconsin.

Listening to bird songs and learning about them is a wonderful way to expand your enjoyment of Wisconsin's birds. The optional *Birds of Wisconsin Audio CDs* contain nearly two hours of songs and calls of the birds in this book, as well as tips and mnemonics for learning the calls.

There are over 800 species of birds found in North America. In Wisconsin alone there have been more than 406 kinds of birds recorded through the years. These bird sightings were diligently recorded by hundreds of bird watchers and became part of the official state record. From these records, I've chosen 111 of the most common birds of Wisconsin to include in this field guide.

Bird watching, often called "birding," is the largest spectator sport in America. Its outstanding popularity in Wisconsin is due, in part, to an unusually rich and abundant birdlife. Why are there so many birds? One reason is open space. Wisconsin is more than 65,400 square miles (170,000 sq. km), making it the twenty-second largest state. Despite its large size, only about 5 million people call Wisconsin their home. On average, that is only 76 people per square mile (29 per sq. km). Approximately three-quarters of all the people in Wisconsin live in or around five major cities in the lower one-half of the state, which leaves plenty of room for a wide variety of birds to roam.

Open space is not the only reason there is such an abundance of birds. It's also the diversity of habitat. The state can be broken into several distinct habitats, each of which supports a different group of birds.

Upper northern Wisconsin is covered with vast stands of evergreen (coniferous) forests, nearly 8,000 lakes and hundreds of miles of streams and rivers. The evergreen woods are havens for Common Ravens, Evening Grosbeaks, Ruby-crowned Kinglets and other birds, while Common Loons and Hooded Mergansers dive for fish in the crystal clear northern lakes.

North of the great forests is the granddaddy of all lakes–Lake Superior, the world's largest freshwater lake. Lake Michigan is on the eastern border of the state. Wisconsin has over 650 miles (1,047 km) of Great Lakes shoreline. The clear cold waters and rocky shores are home to an entirely different group of birds, including Herring Gulls, Ring-billed Gulls and Common Terns.

A vegetation "tension" zone divides the northern coniferous forests from the southern deciduous woods. The division line runs from the western counties of Polk and Burnett, near the area of Minnesota's Twin Cities, south and to the east, ending in Milwaukee County just north of Racine. South of the tension zone is a very different forest type, which attracts different birds. Birds such as Ring-necked Pheasants, Wild Turkeys and Eastern Screech-Owls live here in the oak, maple and elm woods.

The mighty Mississippi River and the St. Croix make up most of Wisconsin's western border. Several other major rivers flow across the state, each lined with shade-producing tall trees. The river valleys are outstanding places for birds. Belted Kingfishers and Green Herons fish in the shallow backwaters there.

Besides the varying habitat, Wisconsin is known for its weather. From the frigid winters to the steamy summers, there are birds to watch in every season. Whether witnessing a migration of hawks in autumn or welcoming back hummingbirds in spring, there is variety and excitement in birding as each season turns to the next.

OBSERVE WITH A STRATEGY; TIPS FOR IDENTIFYING BIRDS

Identifying birds isn't as difficult as you might think. By simply following a few basic strategies, you can increase your chances of successfully identifying most birds you see! One of the first and easiest things to do when you see a new bird is to note its color. (Also, since this book is organized by color, you will go right to that color section to find it.)

Next, note the size of the bird. A strategy to quickly estimate size is to select a small-, medium- and large-sized bird to use for reference. For example, most people are familiar with robins. A robin, measured from tip of the bill to tip of the tail, is 10 inches (25 cm) long. Using the robin as an example of a medium-sized bird, select two other birds, one smaller and one larger. Many people use a House Sparrow, at about 6 inches (15 cm), and an American Crow, about 18 inches (45 cm). When you see a bird that you don't know, you can quickly ask yourself, "Is it smaller than a robin, but larger than a sparrow?" When you look in your field guide to help identify your bird, you'll know it is roughly between 6-10 inches (15-25 cm) long. This will help to narrow your choices.

Next, note the size, shape and color of the bill. Is it long, short, thick, thin, pointed, blunt, curved or straight? Seed-eating birds such as Northern Cardinals have bills that are thick and strong enough to crack even the toughest seeds. Birds that sip nectar such as Ruby-throated Hummingbirds need long thin bills to reach deep into flowers. Hawks and owls tear their prey with very sharp, curving bills. Sometimes, just noting the bill shape can help you decide if the bird is a woodpecker, finch, grosbeak, blackbird or bird of prey.

Next, take a look around and note the habitat in which you see the bird. Is it wading in a marsh? Walking along a riverbank? Soaring in the sky? Is it perched high in the trees or hopping along the forest floor? Because of their preferences in diet and habitat, you'll usually see robins hopping on the ground, but not often eating the seeds at your feeder. Or you will see a Blue Jay sitting on the branches of a tree, but not climbing headfirst down a tree trunk like the White-breasted Nuthatch.

Noticing what a bird is eating will give you another clue to help you identify that bird. Feeding is a big part of any bird's life. Fully one-third of all bird activity revolves around searching for and catching food, or actually eating. While birds don't always follow all the rules of what we think they eat, you can make some general assumptions. Northern Flickers, for instance, feed upon ants and other insects, so you wouldn't expect to see them visiting a backyard feeder. Some birds such as Barn Swallows and Tree Swallows feed upon flying insects and spend hours swooping and diving to catch a meal.

Sometimes you can identify a bird by the way it perches. Body posture can help you differentiate between an American Crow and a Red-tailed Hawk. American Crows lean forward over their feet on a branch, while hawks perch in a vertical position. Look for this the next time you see a large unidentified bird in a tree.

Birds in flight are often difficult to identify, but noting the size and shape of the wing will help. A bird's wing size is in direct proportion to its body size, weight and type of flying. The shape of the wing determines if the bird flies fast and with precision, or slowly and less precisely. Birds such as House Finches, which flit around in thick tangles of branches, have short round wings. Birds that soar on warm updrafts of air, such as Turkey Vultures, have long broad wings. Barn Swallows have short pointed wings that slice through the air, propelling their swift and accurate flight.

Some birds have unique patterns of flight that aid in identification. American Goldfinches fly in a distinctive up-and-down pattern that makes it look as if they are riding a roller coaster.

While it's not easy to make these observations in the short time you often have to watch a "mystery bird," practicing these methods of identification will greatly expand your skills in birding. Also, seek the guidance of a more experienced birder who will help you improve your skills and answer questions on the spot.

Bird Songs and Calls

Another part of bird identification involves using your ears. A song or call can be enough to positively identify a bird without seeing it. If you see a bird that you don't know, the song or call can help you identify it. To learn about bird songs, calls, how they are produced, what they mean and how they are used, see the companion *Birds of Wisconsin Audio CDs*.

BIRD BASICS

It's easier to identify birds and communicate about them if you know the names of the different parts of a bird. For instance, it's more effective to use the word "crest" to indicate the set of extra long feathers on top of a Northern Cardinal's head than to try to describe it.

The following illustration points out the basic parts of a bird. Because it is a composite of many birds, it shouldn't be confused with any actual bird.

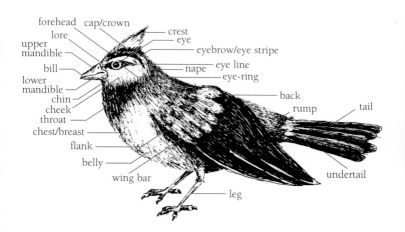

Bird Color Variables

No other animal has a color palette like a bird's. Brilliant blues, lemon yellows, showy reds and iridescent greens are common-place within the bird world. In general, the male birds are more colorful than their female counterparts. This is probably to help the male attract a mate, essentially saying, "Hey, look at me!" It also calls attention to the male's overall health. The better the condition of his feathers, the better his food source and territory, and therefore the better his potential for a mate.

Female birds that don't look like their male counterparts (such species are called sexually dimorphic, meaning "two forms") are often a nondescript color, as seen with the Indigo Bunting. These muted tones help hide the females during weeks of motionless incubation, and draw less attention to them when they are out feeding or taking a break from the rigors of raising their young.

In some species such as the Bald Eagle, Blue Jay and Downy Woodpecker, male birds look nearly identical to the females. In the case of woodpeckers, the sexes are differentiated by only a single red mark or sometimes a yellow mark. Depending upon the species, the mark may be on top of the head, face, nape of neck or just behind the bill.

During the first year, juvenile birds often look like the mothers. Since brightly colored feathers are used mainly for attracting a mate, young non-breeding males don't have a need for colorful plumage. It is not until the first spring molt (or several years later, depending on the species) that young males obtain their breeding colors.

Both breeding and winter plumages are the result of molting. Molting is the process of dropping old worn feathers and replacing them with new ones. All birds molt, typically twice a year, with the spring molt usually occurring in late winter. During this time, most birds produce their breeding plumage (brighter colors for attracting mates), which lasts throughout the summer.

Winter plumage is the result of the late summer molt, which serves a couple of important functions. First, it adds feathers for warmth in the coming winter season. Second, in some species it produces feathers that tend to be drab in color, which helps to camouflage the birds and hide them from predators. The winter plumage of the male American Goldfinch, for example, is olive brown unlike its obvious canary yellow color during summer. Luckily for us, some birds such as the male Northern Cardinal retain their bright summer colors all year long.

Bird Nests

Bird nests are truly an amazing feat of engineering. Imagine building your home strong enough to weather a storm, large enough to hold your entire family, insulated enough to shelter them from cold and heat, and waterproof enough to keep out rain. Now, build it without any blueprints or directions, and without the use of your hands or feet! Birds do!

Before building a nest, an appropriate site must be selected. In some species such as House Wrens, the male picks out several potential sites and assembles several small twigs in each. This discourages other birds from using nearby nest cavities. These "extra" nests are occasionally called dummy nests. The female is then taken around and shown all the choices. She chooses her favorite and finishes constructing the nest. In some other species of birds—Baltimore Orioles, for example—it is the female who chooses the site and constructs the nest, with the male offering only an occasional suggestion. Each species has its own nest-building routine, which is strictly followed.

As you'll see in the following illustrations, birds build a wide variety of nest types.

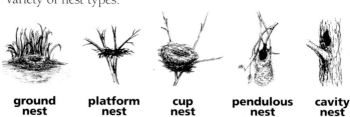

| ground nest | platform nest | cup nest | pendulous nest | cavity nest |

Nesting material often consists of natural elements found in the immediate area. Most nests consist of plant fibers (such as bark peeled from grapevines), sticks, mud, dried grass, feathers, fur, or soft fuzzy tufts from thistle. Some birds, including Ruby-throated Hummingbirds, use spider webs to glue nest materials together. Nesting material is limited to what a bird can hold or carry. Because of this, a bird must make many trips afield to gather enough materials to complete its nest. Most nests take at least four days or more, and hundreds, if not thousands, of trips to build.

The simple **ground nest** is scraped out of the earth. A shallow depression that usually contains no nesting material, it is made by birds such as the Killdeer and Horned Lark.

Another kind of nest, the **platform nest**, represents a more complex type of nest building. Constructed of small twigs and branches, the platform nest is a simple arrangement of sticks which forms a platform and features a small depression to nestle the eggs.

Some platform nests, such as those of the Canada Goose, are constructed on the ground and are made with mud and grass. Platform nests can also be on cliffs, bridges, balconies or even in flowerpots. This kind of nest gives space to adventurous youngsters and functions as a landing platform for the parents. Many waterfowl build platform nests on the ground, usually near water or actually in water. These floating platform nests vary with the water level, thus preventing nests with eggs from being flooded. Platform nests, constructed by such birds as Mourning Doves and herons, are not anchored to the tree and may tumble from the branches during high winds and storms.

The **cup nest** is a modified platform nest, used by three-quarters of all songbirds. Constructed from the outside in, a supporting platform is constructed first. This platform is attached firmly to a tree, shrub, rock ledge or the ground. Next, the sides are constructed of grasses, small twigs, bark or leaves, which are woven together and often glued with mud for added strength. The inner cup, lined with feathers, soft plant material, animal fur or animal hair, is constructed last. The mother bird uses her chest to cast the final contours of the inner nest.

The **pendulous nest** is an unusual nest, looking more like a sock hanging from a branch than a nest. Inaccessible to most predators, these nests are attached to the ends of the smallest branches of a tree and often wave wildly in the breeze. Woven very tightly of plant fibers, they are strong, watertight and take up to a week to construct. More commonly used by tropical birds, this complicated type of nest has also been mastered by orioles and kinglets. A small opening on the top or side allows the parents access to the grass-lined interior. (It must be one heck of a ride to be inside one of these nests during a windy spring thunderstorm!)

Another type of nest, the **cavity nest**, is used by many bird species, including woodpeckers and Eastern Bluebirds. The cavity nest is usually excavated in a tree branch or trunk and offers shelter from storms, sun, predators and cold. A relatively small entrance hole in a tree leads to an inner chamber up to 10 inches (25 cm) below. Usually constructed by woodpeckers, the cavity nest is typically used only once by its builder, but subsequently can be used for many years by birds such as Tree Swallows, mergansers and bluebirds, which do not have the capability of excavating one for themselves. Kingfishers, on the other hand, excavate a tunnel up to 4 feet (1 m) long, which connects the entrance in a riverbank to the nest chamber. These cavity nests are often sparsely lined because they are already well insulated.

Some birds, including some swallows, take nest building one step further. They use a collection of small balls of mud to construct an adobe-style home. Constructed beneath the eaves of houses, under bridges or inside chimneys, some of these nests look like simple cup nests. Others are completely enclosed, with small tunnel-like openings that lead into a safe nesting chamber for the baby birds.

One of the most clever of all nest types is known as the **no nest** or daycare nest. Parasitic birds such as Brown-headed Cowbirds build no nests at all! The egg-laden female expertly searches out other birds' nests and sneaks in to lay one of her own eggs while the host mother is not looking, thereby leaving the host mother to raise an adopted youngster. The mother cowbird wastes no energy building a nest only to have it raided by a predator. By using several nests of other birds, she spreads out her progeny so at least one of her offspring will live to maturity.

Who Builds the Nest?

In general, the female bird builds the nest. She gathers nesting materials and constructs a nest, with an occasional visit from her mate to check on progress. In some species, both parents contribute equally to the construction of a nest. A male bird might forage for precisely the right sticks, grass or mud, but it is often the female that forms or puts together the nest. She uses her body to form the egg chamber. Rarely does the male build a nest by himself.

Fledging

Fledging is the interval between hatching and flight or leaving the nest. Some birds leave the nest within hours of hatching (precocial), but it might be weeks before they are able to fly. This is common with waterfowl and shorebirds. Until they start to fly, they are called fledglings. Birds that are still in the nest are called nestlings. Other baby birds are born naked and blind, and remain in the nest for several weeks (altricial).

Why Birds Migrate

Why do birds migrate? The short answer is simple–food. Birds migrate to areas with high concentrations of food, as it is easier to breed where food is than where it is not. A typical migrating bird–the Scarlet Tanager, for instance–migrates from the tropics of Central and South America to nest in the forests of North America, taking advantage of billions of newly hatched insects to feed its young. This trip is called **complete migration**.

Some birds of prey return from their complete migration to northern regions that are overflowing with small rodents such as mice and voles that have continued to breed in winter.

Complete migrators have a set time and pattern of migration. Each year at nearly the same time, they take off and head for a specific wintering ground. Complete migrators may travel great distances, sometimes as much as 15,000 miles (24,150 km) or more in one year. But complete migration does not necessarily imply flying from the frozen northland to a tropical destination. The Dark-eyed Junco, for example, is a complete migrator that flies from the far reaches of Canada to spend the winter right here in cold and snowy Wisconsin.

There are many interesting aspects to complete migrators. In the spring, males usually migrate several weeks before the females, arriving early to scope out possibilities for nesting sites and food sources, and to begin to defend territories. The females arrive several weeks later. In the autumn, in many species, the females and their young leave early, often up to four weeks before the adult males.

All migrators are not the same type. There are **partial migrators** such as American Goldfinches that usually wait until the food supply dwindles before flying south. Unlike complete migrators, the partial migrators move only far enough south, or sometimes east and west, to find abundant food. In some years it might be only a few hundred miles, while in other years it might be nearly a thousand. This kind of migration, dependent on the weather and available food, is sometimes called **seasonal movement**.

Unlike the predictable ebbing and flowing behavior of complete migrators or partial migrators, **irruptive migrators** can move every third to fifth year or, in some cases, in consecutive years. These migrations are triggered when times are really tough and food is scarce. Red-breasted Nuthatches are a good example of irruptive migrators, because they leave their normal northern range in search of food or in response to overpopulation.

How Do Birds Migrate?

One of the many secrets of migration is fat. While we humans are fighting the battle of the bulge, birds intentionally gorge themselves to put on as much fat as possible while still being able to fly. Fat provides the greatest amount of energy per unit of weight, and in the same way that your car needs gas, birds are propelled by fat and stalled without it.

During long migratory flights, fat deposits are used up quickly, and birds need to stop to "refuel." This is when backyard bird feeding stations and undeveloped, natural spaces around our towns and cities are especially important. Some birds require up to 2-3 days of constant feeding to build their fat reserves before continuing their seasonal trip.

Some birds such as most eagles, hawks, ospreys, falcons and vultures migrate during the day. Larger birds can hold more body fat, go longer without eating and take longer to migrate. These birds glide along on rising columns of warm air, called thermals, which hold them aloft while they slowly make their way north or south. They generally rest during the night and hunt early in the morning before the sun has a chance to warm the land and create good soaring conditions. Birds migrating during the day use a combination of landforms, rivers, and the rising and setting sun to guide them in the right direction.

Most other birds migrate during the night. Studies show that some birds which migrate at night use the stars to navigate. Others use the setting sun, while still others such as doves use the earth's magnetic fields to guide them north or south. While flying at night might seem like a crazy idea, nocturnal migration is safer for several reasons. First, there are fewer nighttime predators for migrating birds. Second, traveling at night allows time during the day to find food in unfamiliar surroundings. Finally, nighttime wind patterns tend to be flat, or laminar. These flat winds don't have the turbulence associated with daytime winds and can actually help carry smaller birds by pushing them along.

HOW TO USE THIS GUIDE

To help you quickly and easily identify birds, this book is organized by color. Simply note the color of the bird and turn to that section. Refer to the first page for the color key. The male Rose-breasted Grosbeak, for example, is black and white with a red patch on its chest. Because the bird is mostly black and white, it will be found in the black and white section. Each color section is also arranged by size, generally with the smaller birds first. Sections may also incorporate the average size in a range, which, in some cases, reflects size differences between the male and female birds. Flip through the pages in that color section to find the bird. If you already know the name of the bird, check the index for the page number. In some species, the male and female are remarkably different in color. In others, the color of the breeding and winter plumages differs. These species have an inset photograph with a page reference and in most cases are found in two color sections.

In the description section you will find a variety of information about the bird. On page xix is a sample of information included in the book.

Range Maps

Range maps are included for each bird. Colored areas indicate where in Wisconsin a particular bird is most likely to be found. The colors represent the presence of a species during a specific season, not the density or amount of birds in the area. Green is used for summer, blue for winter, red for year-round and yellow for areas where the bird is seen during migration. While every effort has been made to accurately depict these ranges, they are only general guidelines. Ranges actually change on an ongoing basis due to a variety of factors. Changes in the weather, species abundance, landscape and vital resources such as availability of food and water can affect local populations, migration and movements, causing birds to be found in areas that are atypical for the species.

Colored areas simply mean bird sightings for that species have been frequent in those areas and less frequent in others. These range boundaries are based on records from *The Passenger Pigeon*, a publication of the Wisconsin Society for Ornithology, *Wisconsin Birdlife* by Samuel D. Robbins, Jr., the Wisconsin Breeding Bird Project, Wisconsin Department of Natural Resources and U.S. Fish and Wildlife Service. Please use the maps as intended–as general guides only.

Using the Companion *Birds of Wisconsin Audio CDs*

The CD icon at the bottom of each description page includes a track number for the bird on the *Birds of Wisconsin Audio CDs*. Play the track number to hear the bird's songs and calls. Bird songs and calls on the CDs are organized in the same order as the birds in the book. For species in which the male and female are different colors (sexually dimorphic), the birds are shown in the book in two color sections. On the CDs the recording of a species is presented only once and coincides with the first time the bird is shown in the book.

Common Name

— Range Map   *Scientific name*   Color Indicator —

YEAR-ROUND
MIGRATION
SUMMER
WINTER

Size: measures head to tail, may include wingspan

Male: a brief description of the male bird, and may include breeding, winter or other plumages

Female: a brief description of the female bird, which is sometimes not the same as the male

Juvenile: a brief description of the juvenile bird, which often looks like the female

Nest: the kind of nest this bird builds to raise its young; who builds the nest; how many broods per year

Eggs: how many eggs you might expect to see in a nest; color and marking

Incubation: the average time parents spend incubating the eggs; who does the incubation

Fledging: the average time young spend in the nest after hatching but before they leave the nest; who does the most "childcare" and feeding

Migration: complete (consistent, seasonal), partial migrator (seasonal, destination varies), irruptive (unpredictable, depends on the food supply), non-migrator; additional comments

Food: what the bird eats most of the time (e.g., seeds, insects, fruit, nectar, small mammals, fish); if it typically comes to a bird feeding station

Compare: notes about other birds that look similar, and the pages on which they can be found

Stan's Notes: Interesting gee-whiz natural history information. This could be something to look or listen for, or something to help positively identify the bird. Also includes remarkable features.

 Track number on *Birds of Wisconsin Audio CDs* (sold separately).   xix

female
pg. 100

male

SUMMER

Eastern Towhee
Pipilo erythrophthalmus

Size: 7-8" (18-20 cm)

Male: A mostly black bird with dirty red brown sides and white belly. Long black tail with white tip. Short, stout, pointed bill and rich red eyes. White wing patches flash in flight.

Female: similar to male, but is brown, not black

Juvenile: light brown, a heavily streaked head, chest and belly, long dark tail with white tip

Nest: cup; female builds; 2 broods per year

Eggs: 3-4; creamy white with brown markings

Incubation: 12-13 days; female incubates

Fledging: 10-12 days; male and female feed young

Migration: complete, to southern states, Mexico and Central and South America

Food: insects, seeds, fruit; visits ground feeders

Compare: Slightly smaller than the American Robin (pg. 190). The Gray Catbird (pg. 188) lacks a black "hood" and rusty sides. Common Grackle (pg. 12) lacks white belly and has long thin bill. Male Rose-breasted Grosbeak (pg. 28) has a rosy patch in center of chest.

Stan's Notes: Common name comes from its distinctive "tow-hee" call given by both sexes. Mostly known for its characteristic call that sounds like, "Drink-your-tea!" Seen hopping backward with both feet (bilateral scratching), raking up leaf litter in search of insects and seeds. The female broods, but the male does the most feeding of young. In southern coastal states, some have red eyes and others have white eyes.

CD 1, TRACK 2

female
pg. 106

male

Brown-headed Cowbird
Molothrus ater

SUMMER

Size: 7½" (19 cm)

Male: A glossy black bird, reminiscent of the Red-winged Blackbird. Chocolate brown head with a pointed, sharp gray bill.

Female: dull brown bird with bill similar to male

Juvenile: similar to female, only dull gray color and a streaked chest

Nest: no nest; lays eggs in nests of other birds

Eggs: 5-7; white with brown markings

Incubation: 10-13 days; host bird incubates eggs

Fledging: 10-11 days; host birds feed young

Migration: complete, to southern states

Food: insects, seeds; will come to seed feeders

Compare: The male Red-winged Blackbird (pg. 8) is slightly larger with red and yellow patches on upper wings. Common Grackle (pg. 12) has a long tail and lacks the brown head. European Starling (pg. 6) has a shorter tail.

Stan's Notes: A member of the blackbird family. Of approximately 750 species of parasitic birds worldwide, this is the only parasitic bird in the state, laying eggs in host birds' nests, leaving others to raise its young. Cowbirds are known to have laid eggs in nests of over 200 species of birds. Some birds reject cowbird eggs, but most incubate them and raise the young, even to the exclusion of their own. Look for warblers and other birds feeding young birds twice their own size. At one time cowbirds followed bison to feed on insects attracted to the animals.

CD 1, TRACK 3

4

winter

breeding

European Starling
Sturnus vulgaris

YEAR-ROUND

Size: 7½" (19 cm)

Male: Gray-to-black bird with white speckles in fall and winter. Shiny purple black during spring and summer. Long, pointed yellow bill in spring turns gray in fall. Short tail.

Female: same as male

Juvenile: similar to adult, gray brown in color with a streaked chest

Nest: cavity; male and female line cavity; 2 broods per year

Eggs: 4-6; bluish with brown markings

Incubation: 12-14 days; female and male incubate

Fledging: 18-20 days; female and male feed young

Migration: non-migrator to partial migrator; some will move to southern states

Food: insects, seeds, fruit; comes to seed and suet feeders

Compare: Similar to Common Grackle (pg. 12), but lacks its long tail. The male Brown-headed Cowbird (pg. 4) has a longer tail.

Stan's Notes: A great songster, this bird can also mimic sounds. Often displaces woodpeckers, chickadees and other cavity-nesting birds. Can be very aggressive and destroy eggs or young of other birds. The bill changes color with the seasons: yellow in spring and gray in autumn. Jaws are designed to be the most powerful when opening, as they pry open crevices to locate hidden insects. Gathers in the hundreds in autumn. Not a native bird, it was introduced to New York City in 1890-91 from Europe.

CD 1, TRACK 4

6

female pg. 116

male

Red-winged Blackbird
Agelaius phoeniceus

SUMMER

Size: 8½" (22 cm)

Male: Jet black bird with red and yellow shoulder patches on upper wings. Pointed black bill.

Female: heavily streaked brown bird with a pointed brown bill and white eyebrows

Juvenile: same as female

Nest: cup; female builds; 2-3 broods per year

Eggs: 3-4; bluish green with brown markings

Incubation: 10-12 days; female incubates

Fledging: 11-14 days; female and male feed young

Migration: complete, to southern states, Mexico and Central America

Food: seeds, insects; will come to seed feeders

Compare: Slightly larger than the male Brown-headed Cowbird (pg. 4), but is less iridescent and lacks Cowbird's brown head. Differs from all blackbirds due to the red and yellow patches on its wings (epaulets).

Stan's Notes: One of the most widespread and numerous birds in the state. It is a sure sign of spring when the Red-winged Blackbirds return to the marshes. Flocks of up to 100,000 birds have been reported. Males return before the females and defend territories by singing from tops of surrounding vegetation. Males repeat call from the tops of cattails while showing off their red and yellow wing bars (epaulets). Females choose mate and usually will nest over shallow water in thick stands of cattails. Red-wingeds feed mostly on seeds in fall and spring, switching to insects during summer.

female
pg. 120

male

SUMMER

Yellow-headed Blackbird
Xanthocephalus xanthocephalus

Size: 9-11" (22.5-28 cm)

Male: Large black bird with a lemon yellow head, chest and nape of neck. Black mask and a gray bill. White wing patches.

Female: similar to male, only slightly smaller with a brown body, dull yellow head and chest

Juvenile: similar to female

Nest: cup; female builds; 2 broods per year

Eggs: 3-5; greenish white with brown markings

Incubation: 11-13 days; female incubates

Fledging: 9-12 days; female feeds young

Migration: complete, to southern states and Mexico

Food: insects, seeds; will come to ground feeders

Compare: Larger than the male Red-winged Blackbird (pg. 8), which has red and yellow patches on its wings. Male Yellow-headed Blackbird is the only large black bird with a bright yellow head.

Stan's Notes: Usually heard before seen, Yellow-headed Blackbird has a low, hoarse, raspy or metallic call. Nests in deep water marshes unlike its cousin, the Red-winged Blackbird, which prefers shallow water. The male gives an impressive mating display, flying with head drooped and feet and tail pointing down while steadily beating its wings. The female incubates alone and feeds 3-5 young. Young keep low and out of sight for as many as three weeks before starting to fly. Migrates in flocks of up to 200 with other blackbirds. Flocks made up mainly of males return first in April; females return later. Most colonies consist of 20-100 nests.

Common Grackle
Quiscalus quiscula

SUMMER

Size: 11-13" (28-33 cm)

Male: Large black bird with iridescent blue black head, purple brown body, long black tail, long thin bill and bright golden eyes.

Female: similar to male, only duller and smaller

Juvenile: similar to female

Nest: cup; female builds; 2 broods per year

Eggs: 4-5; greenish white with brown markings

Incubation: 13-14 days; female incubates

Fledging: 16-20 days; female and male feed young

Migration: complete, to southern states

Food: fruit, seeds, insects; comes to seed feeders

Compare: European Starling (pg. 6) is much smaller with a speckled appearance, and yellow bill during the breeding season. The male Red-winged Blackbird (pg. 8) has red and yellow wing markings.

Stan's Notes: Usually nests in small colonies of up to 75 pairs, but travels with other blackbirds in large flocks. Is known to feed in farmers' fields. Male holds tail in a vertical keel-like position during flight. The flight pattern is almost always level, as opposed to an undulating up-and-down movement. Unlike most birds, it has larger muscles for opening the mouth (rather than for closing it) and prying crevices apart to locate hidden insects. The name is derived from the Latin word *graculus*, meaning "to cough," for its loud raspy call.

American Coot
Fulica americana

YEAR-ROUND
SUMMER

Size: 13-16" (33-40 cm)

Male: Slate gray to black all over. White bill with dark band near tip. Green legs and feet. A small white patch near the base of the tail. Prominent red eyes. Small red patch above bill between eyes.

Female: same as male

Juvenile: much paler than adult, with a gray bill and same white rump patch

Nest: cup; female and male build; 1 brood per year

Eggs: 9-12; pinkish buff with brown markings

Incubation: 21-25 days; female and male incubate

Fledging: 49-52 days; female and male feed young

Migration: complete, to southern states, Mexico and Central America

Food: insects, aquatic plants

Compare: Smaller than most waterfowl, it is the only black water bird or duck-like bird with a white bill.

Stan's Notes: An excellent diver and swimmer, often seen in large flocks on open water. Not a duck, as it doesn't have webbed feet, but instead has large lobed toes. When taking off, scrambles across surface of water with wings flapping. Bobs head while swimming. Anchors its floating nest to plants. Huge flocks of as many as 1,000 birds gather for migration. The unusual common name "Coot" is of unknown origin, but in Middle English, *coote* was used to describe various waterfowl–perhaps it stuck. Also called Mud Hen.

YEAR-ROUND

American Crow
Corvus brachyrhynchos

Size: 18" (45 cm)

Male: All-black bird with black bill, legs and feet. Can have a purple sheen in direct sunlight.

Female: same as male

Juvenile: same as adult

Nest: platform; female builds; 1 brood per year

Eggs: 4-6; bluish to olive green, brown markings

Incubation: 18 days; female incubates

Fledging: 28-35 days; female and male feed young

Migration: non-migrator to partial migrator

Food: fruit, insects, mammals, fish, carrion; will come to seed and suet feeders

Compare: Similar to the Common Raven (pg. 18), but Crow has a smaller bill, lacks shaggy throat feathers and has a higher-pitched call than Raven's deep, low raspy call. The Crow has a squared tail. Raven has a wedge-shaped tail, apparent in flight.

Stan's Notes: One of the most recognizable birds in Wisconsin. Often reuses its nest every year if not taken over by a Great Horned Owl. Collects and stores bright, shiny objects in the nest. Able to mimic other birds and human voices. One of the smartest of all birds and very social, often entertaining itself by provoking chases with other birds. Feeds on road kill but is rarely hit by cars. Can live up to 20 years. Unmated birds known as helpers help raise the young. Large extended families roost together at night, dispersing during the day to hunt.

CD 1, TRACK 9

16

in flight

YEAR-ROUND

Common Raven
Corvus corax

Size: 22-27" (56-69 cm)

Male: Large all-black bird with a large black bill, a shaggy beard of feathers on the chin and throat, and a large wedge-shaped tail, seen in flight.

Female: same as male

Juvenile: same as adult

Nest: platform; female and male build; 1 brood per year

Eggs: 4-6; pale green with brown markings

Incubation: 18-21 days; female incubates

Fledging: 38-44 days; female and male feed young

Migration: non-migrator to partial migrator

Food: insects, fruit, small animals, carrion

Compare: Larger than its cousin, the American Crow (pg. 16), which lacks the throat patch of feathers. Glides on flat, outstretched wings unlike the slightly V-shaped pattern of the Crow. Low, raspy call distinguishes Raven from the higher-pitched Crow.

Stan's Notes: This bird is the symbol of Wisconsin's North Woods. Considered by some to be the smartest of all birds. Known for its aerial acrobatics and long swooping dives. Scavenges with crows and gulls. Known to follow wolf packs around to pick up scraps and pick at bones of a kill. Complex courtship includes grabbing bills, preening each other and cooing. Most begin to breed at 3-4 years. Mates for life. Uses the same nest site for many years.

CD 1, TRACK 10

soaring

Turkey Vulture
Cathartes aura

Size: 26-32" (66-80 cm); up to 6-foot wingspan

Male: Large bird with obvious red head and legs. In flight, the wings appear two-toned: black leading edge with gray on the trailing edge and tip. The tips of wings end in finger-like projections. Long squared tail. Ivory bill.

Female: same as male

Juvenile: similar to adult, with gray-to-blackish head and bill

Nest: no nest, or minimal nest on cliff or in cave; 1 brood per year

Eggs: 2; white with brown markings

Incubation: 38-41 days; female and male incubate

Fledging: 66-88 days; female and male feed young

Migration: complete, to southern states, Mexico and Central and South America

Food: carrion; parents regurgitate for young

Compare: Smaller than the Bald Eagle (pg. 50), look for Vulture's two-toned wings. Flies holding wings in a slight V shape unlike the Eagle's straight wing position.

Stan's Notes: The vulture's naked head is an adaptation to reduce risk of feather fouling (picking up diseases) from carcasses. Unlike hawks and eagles, it has weak feet more suited to walking than grasping. One of the few birds that has a developed sense of smell. Mostly mute, making only grunts and groans. Seen in trees with wings outstretched to catch sun. Recent studies show this bird is closely related to storks, not birds of prey.

MUTE (not on CD)

in flight

juvenile

crests

drying

Double-crested Cormorant

Phalacrocorax auritus

MIGRATION
SUMMER

Size: 33" (84 cm); up to 4½-foot wingspan

Male: A large black water bird with a long snake-like neck. Two crests on head. Long gray bill with yellow at the base and a hooked tip.

Female: same as male

Juvenile: lighter brown with a grayish chest and neck

Nest: platform, in colony; male and female build; 1 brood per year

Eggs: 3-4; bluish white without markings

Incubation: 25-29 days; female and male incubate

Fledging: 37-42 days; male and female feed young

Migration: complete, to southern states, Mexico and Central America

Food: small fish, aquatic insects

Compare: Similar size as the Turkey Vulture (pg. 20), which also perches on branches with wings open to dry in sun, but Vulture has a naked red head. Twice the size of American Coot (pg. 14), which lacks the Cormorant's long neck and long pointed bill.

Stan's Notes: Often seen flying in large V formation. Usually roosts in large groups in trees close to water. Catches fish by swimming underwater with wings held at its sides. Lacks the oil gland that keeps feathers from becoming waterlogged. To dry off it strikes an erect pose with wings outstretched, facing the sun. Common name refers to the two crests on its head, which are not usually seen. "Cormorant" comes from the Latin words *corvus,* meaning "crow," and *L. marinus*, meaning "pertaining to the sea," literally, "Sea Crow."

male

female

Black-and-white Warbler

Mniotilta varia

MIGRATION
SUMMER

Size: 5" (13 cm)

Male: Striped like a zebra, this small warbler has a distinctive black-and-white striped cap. White belly. Black chin and cheek patch.

Female: same as male, only duller and without the black chin and cheek patch

Juvenile: similar to female

Nest: cup; female builds; 1 brood per year

Eggs: 4-5; white with brown markings

Incubation: 10-11 days; female incubates

Fledging: 9-12 days; female and male feed young

Migration: complete, to Florida, Mexico, Central and South America

Food: insects

Compare: Look for Warbler to creep down tree trunks headfirst, like the Red-breasted and White-breasted Nuthatches (pp. 170 and 178). Brown Creeper (pg. 68) is brown and white and has a longer, downward curving bill.

Stan's Notes: This is one of the first warblers to return in spring. The only warbler that moves headfirst down a tree trunk. Look for it searching for insect eggs in the bark of large trees. Song sounds like a slowly turning, squeaky wheel. Female performs a distraction dance to draw predators away from the nest. Makes its nest on the ground, concealed under dead leaves or at the base of a tree.

male

female

Downy Woodpecker
Picoides pubescens

Size: 6" (15 cm)

Male: A small woodpecker with an all-white belly, black-and-white spotted wings, a black line running through the eyes, a short black bill, a white stripe down the back and red mark on the back of the head. Several small black spots along the sides of white tail.

Female: same as male, but lacks a red mark on head

Juvenile: same as female, some have a red mark near the forehead

Nest: cavity; male and female excavate; 1 brood per year

Eggs: 3-5; white without markings

Incubation: 11-12 days; female and male incubate, the female during day, male at night

Fledging: 20-25 days; male and female feed young

Migration: non-migrator

Food: insects, seeds; visits seed and suet feeders

Compare: Almost identical to the Hairy Woodpecker (pg. 32), but smaller. Look for the shorter, thinner bill of Downy to differentiate them.

Stan's Notes: Abundant and widespread where trees are present. Stiff tail feathers help brace it like a tripod as it clings to a tree. Like all woodpeckers, it has a long barbed tongue to pull insects from tiny places. Male and female will drum on branches or hollow logs to announce territories, which are rarely larger than 5 acres (2 ha). Male performs most brooding. Will winter roost in cavity.

female
pg. 110

male

Rose-breasted Grosbeak
Pheucticus ludovicianus

SUMMER

Size: 7-8" (18-20 cm)

Male: A plump black-and-white bird with a large, triangular rose patch in the center of chest. Wing linings are rosy red. Large ivory bill.

Female: heavily streaked brown and white bird with large white eyebrows, orange yellow wing linings

Juvenile: similar to female

Nest: cup; female and male construct; 1-2 broods per year

Eggs: 3-5; blue green with brown markings

Incubation: 13-14 days; female and male incubate

Fledging: 9-12 days; female and male feed young

Migration: complete, to Mexico, Central America and South America

Food: insects, seeds, fruit; comes to seed feeders

Compare: Male is very distinctive with no look-alikes.

Stan's Notes: Summer resident throughout the state. Often prefers mature deciduous forest for nesting. Both sexes sing, but the male sings much louder and clearer. Has a rich, robin-like song. The name "Grosbeak" refers to its large bill, used to crush seeds. Rose breast patch varies in size and shape in each male. Late to arrive in spring and early to leave in autumn. Males arrive in small groups first, joined by females several days later. Several males can be seen visiting seed feeders at the same time in spring. When the females arrive, males become territorial and reduce their visits to feeders. Young grosbeaks visit feeders with adults after fledging.

male

female

Yellow-bellied Sapsucker
Sphyrapicus varius

MIGRATION
SUMMER

Size: 8-9" (20-22.5 cm)

Male: Medium-sized woodpecker with checkered back. Has a red forehead, crown and chin. Tan-to-yellow breast and belly. White wing patches flash while flying.

Female: similar to male, white chin

Juvenile: similar to female, dull brown and lacks any red marking

Nest: cavity; female and male excavate; 1 brood per year

Eggs: 5-6; white without markings

Incubation: 12-13 days; female and male incubate, the female during day, male at night

Fledging: 25-29 days; female and male feed young

Migration: complete, to southern states, Mexico and Central America

Food: insects, tree sap; comes to suet feeders

Compare: The male Yellow-bellied Sapsucker shares the red chin of Red-headed Woodpecker (pg. 34), but lacks an all-red head. Female Yellow-bellied Sapsucker has a white chin.

Stan's Notes: Drills holes in a pattern of horizontal rows in small-to medium-sized trees to bleed tree sap. Many birds drink from sapsucker taps. Oozing sap also attracts insects, which sapsuckers eat. Sapsuckers will defend their sapping sites from the other birds. They don't suck sap; rather, they lap it with their long tongues. A quiet bird with few vocalizations, but will mew like a cat. Unlike other woodpeckers, drumming rhythm is irregular.

CD 1, TRACK 15

male

female

Hairy Woodpecker
Picoides villosus

Size: 9" (22.5 cm)

Male: Black-and-white woodpecker with a white belly, and black wings with rows of white spots. White stripe down back. Long black bill. Red mark on back of head.

Female: same as male, but lacks a red mark on head

Juvenile: grayer version of female

Nest: cavity; female and male excavate; 1 brood per year

Eggs: 3-6; white without markings

Incubation: 11-15 days; female and male incubate, the female during day, male at night

Fledging: 28-30 days; male and female feed young

Migration: non-migrator

Food: insects, nuts, seeds; comes to seed and suet feeders

Compare: Larger than Downy Woodpecker (pg. 26), Hairy has a longer bill and lacks Downy's black spots along tail.

Stan's Notes: A common woodpecker of wooded backyards that announces its arrival with a sharp chirp before landing on feeders. This bird is responsible for eating many destructive forest insects. Has a barbed tongue, which helps it extract insects from trees. Tiny bristle-like feathers at the base of bill protect the nostrils from wood dust. Drums on hollow logs, branches or stovepipes in springtime to announce its territory. Often prefers to excavate nest cavities in live aspen trees. Has a larger, more oval-shaped cavity entrance than that of Downy Woodpecker.

CD 1, TRACK 16

Red-headed Woodpecker
Melanerpes erythrocephalus

SUMMER

Size: 9" (22.5 cm)

Male: All-red head and a solid black back. White rump, chest and belly. Large white patches on wings flash when in flight. A black tail. Gray legs and bill.

Female: same as male

Juvenile: gray brown with white chest, lacks any red

Nest: cavity; male builds with help from female; 1 brood per year

Eggs: 4-5; white without markings

Incubation: 12-13 days; female and male incubate

Fledging: 27-30 days; female and male feed young

Migration: partial to complete; will move to areas with an abundant supply of nuts

Food: insects, nuts, fruit; comes to seed and suet feeders

Compare: No other woodpecker in Wisconsin has an all-red head. Pileated Woodpecker (pg. 42) is the only other woodpecker with a solid black back, but it has a partial red head.

Stan's Notes: One of the few woodpecker species in which male and female appear the same (look alike). Bill is not as well adapted for excavating holes as in other woodpeckers, so it chooses dead or rotten tree branches for nest. Later nesting than the closely related Red-bellied Woodpecker and will often take over its nesting cavity. Prefers more open or edge woodlands with many dead trees. Often seen perching on tops of dead snags. Stores acorns and other nuts. Nationwide populations are on the decrease.

male

female

YEAR-ROUND

Red-bellied Woodpecker
Melanerpes carolinus

Size: 9¼" (23 cm)

Male: "Zebra-backed" woodpecker with a white rump. Red crown extends down the nape of neck. Tan breast with a tinge of red on belly, which is often hard to see.

Female: same as male, but with a gray crown

Juvenile: gray version of adults, no red cap or nape

Nest: cavity; female and male excavate; 1 brood per year

Eggs: 4-5; white without markings

Incubation: 12-14 days; female and male incubate, the female during day, male at night

Fledging: 24-27 days; female and male feed young

Migration: non-migrator; moves around to find food

Food: insects, nuts, fruit; comes to seed and suet feeders

Compare: Similar to Northern Flicker (pg. 130) and Yellow-bellied Sapsucker (pg. 30). Note the tan chest and belly with obvious black-and-white stripes on the back. The Red-headed Woodpecker (pg. 34) has an all-red head.

Stan's Notes: Named for its easily overlooked rosy red belly patch. Mostly a bird of shady woodlands, it excavates holes in rotten wood looking for spiders, centipedes and beetles. Hammers acorns and berries into crevices of trees for winter food. Will return to same tree to excavate a new nest below that of the previous year. Often kicked out of nest hole by European Starlings. Gives a loud "querrr" call and a low "chug-chug-chug."

female pg. 136

male

Bufflehead
Bucephala albeola

MIGRATION
WINTER

Size: 13-15" (33-38 cm)

Male: A small duck with striking white sides and black back. Green purple head with a large white bonnet-like patch.

Female: brown version of male, with a brown head and white patch on cheek, just behind eyes

Juvenile: similar to female

Nest: cavity; female lines old woodpecker cavity; 1 brood per year

Eggs: 8-10; ivory to olive without markings

Incubation: 29-31 days; female incubates

Fledging: 50-55 days; female leads young to food

Migration: complete, to the shores of Lake Michigan and the Mississippi River, southern states, Mexico and Central America

Food: aquatic insects

Compare: The male Common Goldeneye (pg. 44) is slightly larger, shares the white sides and black back, but lacks the white head patch. Male Hooded Merganser (pg. 40) is similar, but lacks the male Bufflehead's white sides.

Stan's Notes: Common diving duck that travels with other ducks. Seen on rivers and lakes. Nests in old woodpecker cavities. Unlike other ducks, the young remain in the nest for up to two days before venturing out with their mother. Female is very territorial and stays with the same mate for many years.

CD 1, TRACK 19

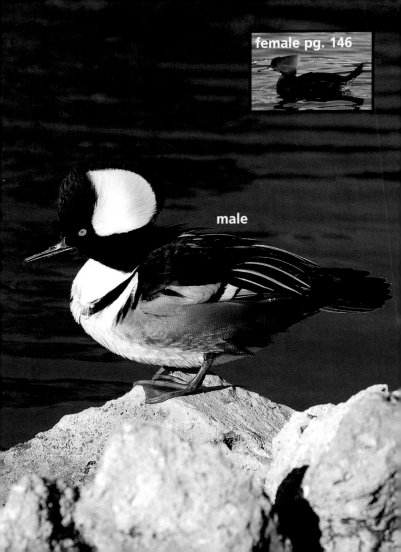

female pg. 146

male

Hooded Merganser
Lophodytes cucullatus

MIGRATION
SUMMER
WINTER

Size: 16-19" (40-48 cm)

Male: A sleek black-and-white bird that has rusty brown sides. Crest "hood" raises to reveal a large white patch. Long, thin black bill.

Female: sleek brown and rust bird with a ragged rusty crest and long, thin brown bill

Juvenile: similar to female

Nest: cavity; female lines old woodpecker hole; 1 brood per year

Eggs: 10-12; white without markings

Incubation: 32-33 days; female incubates

Fledging: 71 days; female feeds young

Migration: complete, to southern states

Food: small fish, aquatic insects

Compare: A distinctive diving bird. Smaller than male Common Merganser (pg. 218). Look for the male's large white patch on the head and rusty brown sides. The male Bufflehead (pg. 38) is smaller and has white sides. Male Wood Duck (pg. 214) has a green head.

Stan's Notes: A small diving bird of shallow ponds, sloughs, lakes and rivers. Male Hooded Merganser can voluntarily raise and lower its crest to show off the large white head patch. Rarely found away from wooded areas, where it nests in natural cavities or nest boxes. Female will "dump" her eggs into other female Hooded Merganser nests, resulting in 20-25 eggs in some nests. Known to share nest cavities with Common Goldeneyes and Wood Ducks, sitting side by side. Not as common as the Common Merganser.

male

female

Pileated Woodpecker
Dryocopus pileatus

YEAR-ROUND

Size: 19" (48 cm)

Male: Crow-sized woodpecker with a black back and bright red crest. Long gray bill with red mustache. White leading edge of the wings flashes brightly when flying.

Female: same as male, but has a black forehead and lacks red mustache

Juvenile: similar to adults, only duller and browner

Nest: cavity; male and female excavate; 1 brood per year

Eggs: 3-5; white without markings

Incubation: 15-18 days; female and male incubate, the female during day, male at night

Fledging: 26-28 days; female and male feed young

Migration: non-migrator

Food: insects; will come to suet feeders

Compare: Red-headed Woodpecker (pg. 34) is about half the size and has an all-red head, black back and white rump. Look for the bright red crest and exceptionally large size of the Pileated Woodpecker.

Stan's Notes: Our largest woodpecker. The common name comes from the Latin *pileatus*, which means "wearing a cap," referring to its crest. A relatively shy bird that prefers large tracts of woodland. Drums on hollow branches, chimneys, etc., to announce territory. Excavates oval holes up to several feet long in tree trunks, looking for insects to eat. Large chips of wood lie at bases of excavated trees. Favorite food is carpenter ants. Young are fed regurgitated insects.

 CD 1, TRACK 21

male

female pg. 150

Common Goldeneye
Bucephala clangula

MIGRATION
SUMMER
WINTER

Size: 18½-20" (47-50 cm)

Male: A mostly white duck with a black back and large, puffy green head. Large white spot in front of each bright golden eye. Dark bill.

Female: brown and gray, a large dark brown head, gray body, white collar, bright golden eyes, yellow-tipped dark bill

Juvenile: same as female, but has a dark bill

Nest: cavity; female lines old woodpecker cavity; 1 brood per year

Eggs: 8-10; light green without markings

Incubation: 28-32 days; female incubates

Fledging: 56-59 days; female leads young to food

Migration: complete, to southwestern Wisconsin along the Mississippi River, southern states and Mexico

Food: aquatic plants, insects

Compare: Larger than the male Bufflehead (pg. 38), which shares the white sides and black back, but has a white bonnet-like patch on the head. Look for a distinctive white mark in front of each golden eye.

Stan's Notes: Known for its loud whistling, produced by its wings in flight. In late winter and early spring, male often attracts female through elaborate displays, throwing its head backward while it utters a single raspy note. Female will lay eggs in other goldeneye nests, which results in some mothers incubating up to 30 eggs. Received the common name from its obvious bright golden eyes.

soaring

MIGRATION
SUMMER

Osprey
Pandion haliaetus

Size: 24" (60 cm); up to 5½-foot wingspan

Male: Large eagle-like bird with a white chest and belly, and a nearly black back. White head with a black streak through the eyes. Large wings with black "wrist" marks. Dark bill.

Female: same as male, but larger with a necklace of brown streaking

Juvenile: similar to adults, with a light tan breast

Nest: platform, often on raised wooden platform; female and male build; 1 brood per year

Eggs: 2-4; white with brown markings

Incubation: 32-42 days; female and male incubate

Fledging: 48-58 days; male and female feed young

Migration: complete, to southern states, Mexico and Central and South America

Food: fish

Compare: Bald Eagle (pg. 50) is on average 10 inches (25 cm) larger with an all-white head and tail. The juvenile Bald Eagle is brown with white speckles. Look for a white belly and dark stripe through eyes to identify Osprey.

Stan's Notes: Ospreys are in a family all their own. It is the only raptor that plunges into water feet first to catch fish. Can hover for a few seconds before diving. Carries fish in a head-first position for better aerodynamics. Often harassed by Bald Eagles for its catch. In flight, wings are angled (cocked) backward. Nests on man-made towers and in tall dead trees. Recent studies show male and female might mate for life. May not migrate to same wintering grounds.

breeding

winter

Common Loon
Gavia immer

Size: 28-36" (71-90 cm)

Male: Large, familiar black-and-white bird of the lakes. The breeding adult has checkerboard back with white necklace, black head and deep red eyes with long, pointed black bill. Winter has an entirely gray body and bill.

Female: same as male

Juvenile: similar to winter adult, lacks red eyes

Nest: platform, on the ground; female and male build; 1 brood per year

Eggs: 2; olive brown, occasionally brown markings

Incubation: 26-31 days; female and male incubate

Fledging: 75-80 days; female and male feed young

Migration: complete, to southern states, the Gulf coast and Mexico

Food: fish, aquatic insects

Compare: Double-crested Cormorant (pg. 22) has a black chest and gray bill with yellow at the base and a hooked tip.

Stan's Notes: A true symbol of the wildness of our lakes. Prefers clear lakes because it hunts for fish by eyesight. Legs are set so far back that it has a difficult time walking on land, but it is a great swimmer. Common name comes from the Swedish word *lom*, meaning "lame," for the awkward way it walks on land. Its unique call suggests the wild laughter of a demented person, and led to the phrase "crazy as a loon." Young ride on backs of swimming parents. Adults perform distraction displays to protect young. Very sensitive to disturbance during nesting and will abandon nest.

soaring

juvenile

soaring
juvenile

Bald Eagle
Haliaeetus leucocephalus

MIGRATION
SUMMER
WINTER

Size: 31-37" (79-94 cm); up to 7-foot wingspan

Male: Pure white head and tail contrast with dark brown-to-black body and wings. A large, curved yellow bill and yellow feet.

Female: same as male, only slightly larger

Juvenile: dark brown with white spots or speckles throughout body and wings, gray bill

Nest: massive platform, usually in a tree; female and male build; 1 brood per year

Eggs: 2; off-white without markings

Incubation: 34-36 days; female and male incubate

Fledging: 75-90 days; female and male feed young

Migration: partial; many winter along the Mississippi River in west central Wisconsin, the rest migrate to southeastern states

Food: fish, carrion, birds (mainly ducks)

Compare: Vulture (pg. 20) lacks adult Eagle's white head and tail. Vulture has two-toned wings and flies with its wings in a V shape unlike the straight-out wing position of the Eagle.

Stan's Notes: Driven to near extinction due to DDT poisoning and illegal killing. Now making a comeback in North America. Returns to same nest each year, adding more sticks, enlarging it to massive proportions, at times up to 1,000 pounds (450 kg). In the midair mating ritual, one eagle will flip upside down and lock talons with another. Both tumble, then break apart to continue flight. Thought to mate for life, but will switch mates if not successful reproducing. Juvenile attains the white head and tail at about 4-5 years of age.

Tree Swallow
Tachycineta bicolor

Size: 5-6" (13-15 cm)

Male: Blue green in the spring and greener in fall. Appears to change color in direct sunlight. A white belly, a notched tail and pointed wing tips.

Female: similar to male, only duller

Juvenile: gray brown with a white belly and grayish breast band

Nest: cavity; female and male line former woodpecker cavity or nest box; 1 brood per year

Eggs: 4-6; white without markings

Incubation: 13-16 days; female incubates

Fledging: 20-24 days; female and male feed young

Migration: complete, to Mexico and Central America

Food: insects

Compare: Similar color as Purple Martin (pg. 60), but smaller with a white breast and belly. The Barn Swallow (pg. 56) has a rust belly and deeply forked tail.

Stan's Notes: The first swallow species to return each spring. Most common along ponds, lakes and agricultural fields. Is attracted to your yard with a nesting box. Competes with Eastern Bluebirds for cavities and nesting boxes. Travels great distances to find dropped feathers to line its grass nest. Sometimes seen playing, chasing after dropped feathers. Often seen flying back and forth across fields, feeding on insects. Gathers in large flocks to migrate.

female pg. 86

male

Indigo Bunting
Passerina cyanea

SUMMER

Size: 5½" (14 cm)

Male: Vibrant blue finch-like bird. Scattered dark markings on wings and tail.

Female: light brown bird with faint markings

Juvenile: similar to female

Nest: cup; female builds; 2 broods per year

Eggs: 3-4; pale blue without markings

Incubation: 12-13 days; female incubates

Fledging: 10-11 days; female feeds young

Migration: complete, to southern Florida, Mexico and Central and South America

Food: insects, seeds, fruit; will visit seed feeders

Compare: Smaller than male Eastern Bluebird (pg. 58) and lacks Bluebird's rusty red breast.

Stan's Notes: Usually only the males are noticed. Actually a black bird, as it doesn't have any blue pigment in its feathers. As with the Blue Jay, sunlight is refracted within the structure of the bunting's feathers, making them appear blue. Appears iridescent in direct sun. Molts to acquire body feathers with gray tips, which quickly wear off to reveal bright blue plumage in spring. Molts in fall to appear like females during winter. Males often sing from treetops to attract mates. Will come to feeders in spring before insects are plentiful. Mostly seen along woodland edges, feeding on insects. Migrates at night in flocks of 5-10 birds. Males return before the females and juveniles, usually returning to previous year's nest site. Juveniles move to within a mile from birth site.

Barn Swallow
Hirundo rustica

SUMMER

Size: 7" (18 cm)

Male: A sleek swallow with a blue black back, a cinnamon belly and a reddish brown chin. White spots on long forked tail.

Female: same as male, only slightly duller

Juvenile: similar to adults, with a tan belly and chin, and shorter tail

Nest: cup; female and male construct; 2 broods per year

Eggs: 4-5; white with brown markings

Incubation: 13-17 days; female incubates

Fledging: 18-23 days; female and male feed young

Migration: complete, to South America

Food: insects, prefers beetles, wasps and flies

Compare: Tree Swallow (pg. 52) has a white belly and chin and a notched tail. The Chimney Swift (pg. 70) has narrow pointed tail with wings longer than the body. The Purple Martin (pg. 60) is nearly 2 inches (5 cm) larger and has a dark purple belly.

Stan's Notes: Of the six swallow species in Wisconsin, this is the only one with a deeply forked tail. Unlike other swallows, Barn Swallow rarely glides in flight, so look for continuous flapping. It builds a mud nest using up to 1,000 beak-loads of mud, often in or on barns. Nests in colonies of 4-6 individuals, but nesting alone isn't uncommon. Drinks in flight, skimming water or getting water from wet leaves. Also bathes while flying through rain or sprinklers.

Eastern Bluebird
Sialia sialis

Size: 7" (18 cm)

Male: Reminiscent of its larger cousin, American Robin, with a rusty red breast and a white belly. Sky blue head, back and tail.

Female: shares rusty red breast and white belly, but is grayer with faint blue tail and wings

Juvenile: similar to female, with spots on chest, blue wing markings

Nest: cavity, old woodpecker cavity or man-made nest box; female builds; 2 broods per year

Eggs: 4-5; pale blue without markings

Incubation: 12-14 days; female incubates

Fledging: 15-18 days; male and female feed young

Migration: complete, to southern states

Food: insects, fruit

Compare: Male Indigo Bunting (pg. 54) is nearly all blue, lacking the rusty red breast. Blue Jay (pg. 62) is much larger and has a crest.

Stan's Notes: Once nearly eliminated from Wisconsin due to a lack of nest cavities, bluebirds have made a remarkable comeback with the aid of bird enthusiasts who have put up thousands of bluebird nest boxes. Easily tamed, will come to a shallow dish with mealworms. Bluebirds like open habitats such as fields, pastures and roadsides. Will perch in trees or on fence posts and wait for grasshoppers. Sings a distinctive "chur-lee chur chur-lee." Gathers in large family groups to migrate. Males return first in springtime, followed by females a week or two later. Young of first brood help raise young of second.

Purple Martin
Progne subis

SUMMER

Size: 8½" (22 cm)

Male: A large swallow-shaped bird with a purple head, back and belly. Black wings and tail. Notched tail.

Female: gray purple head and back with a whitish belly, darker wings and tail

Juvenile: same as female

Nest: cavity; female and male line cavity of house; 1 brood per year

Eggs: 4-5; white without markings

Incubation: 15-18 days; female incubates

Fledging: 26-30 days; male and female feed young

Migration: complete, to South America

Food: insects

Compare: The male is the only swallow with a dark purple belly. Usually seen only in groups.

Stan's Notes: The largest swallow species in North America. Once nested in tree cavities in Wisconsin, but now nearly exclusively nests in man-made nesting boxes. Main diet consists of dragonflies, not mosquitoes as once thought. Often drinks and bathes while flying by skimming water or flying through rain. Returns to the same nest site each year. Males arrive before the females and yearlings. Often nests within 100 feet (30 m) of a human dwelling and, in fact, the most successful colonies are located within this distance. Young strike out to form new colonies. Huge colonies gather in the fall to migrate to South America.

YEAR-ROUND

Blue Jay
Cyanocitta cristata

Size: 12" (30 cm)

Male: Large, bright light blue and white bird with a black necklace. Crest moves up and down at will. White face with a gray belly. White wing bars on blue wings. Black spots and a white tip on blue tail.

Female: same as male

Juvenile: same as adult, only duller

Nest: cup; female and male construct; 1-2 broods per year

Eggs: 4-5; green to blue with brown markings

Incubation: 16-18 days; female incubates

Fledging: 17-21 days; female and male feed young

Migration: non-migrator to partial migrator; will move around to find an abundant food source

Food: insects, fruit, carrion, seeds, nuts; comes to seed feeders, and ground feeders with corn

Compare: Gray Jay (pg. 194) has a similar size, but lacks the crest. Eastern Bluebird (pg. 58) is much smaller and lacks white marks and a crest. Belted Kingfisher (pg. 64) lacks the vivid blue colors and black necklace.

Stan's Notes: Highly intelligent bird, solving problems, gathering food and communicating more than other birds. Will scream like a hawk to scatter birds at a feeder. Known as the alarm of the forest, screaming at intruders in woods. Known to eat eggs or young birds from the nests of other birds. One of the few birds to cache food. Feathers don't have blue pigment; refracted sunlight casts blue light.

male

female

Belted Kingfisher
Ceryle alcyon

Size: 13" (33 cm)

Male: Large blue bird with white belly. Broad blue gray breast band and a ragged crest that is raised and lowered at will. Large head with a long, thick black bill. A small white spot directly in front of red brown eyes. Black wing tips with splashes of white that flash when flying.

Female: same as male, but with rusty breast band in addition to blue gray band, and rusty flanks

Juvenile: similar to female

Nest: cavity; female and male excavate; 1 brood per year

Eggs: 6-7; white without markings

Incubation: 23-24 days; female and male incubate

Fledging: 23-24 days; female and male feed young

Migration: complete, to southern states, Mexico and Central and South America

Food: small fish

Compare: Kingfisher is darker blue than the Blue Jay (pg. 62) and has a larger, more ragged crest. Kingfisher is rarely found away from water.

Stan's Notes: Seen perched on branches near the water, it dives headfirst for small fish and returns to a branch to eat. Has a loud machine-gun-like call. Excavates a deep cavity in bank of river or lake. Parents drop dead fish into water, teaching the young to dive. Regurgitates pellets of bone after meals, being unable to pass bones through digestive tract. Mates recognize each other by call.

Chestnut-sided Warbler
Dendroica pensylvanica

MIGRATION
SUMMER

Size: 5" (13 cm)

Male: A colorful combination of a yellow cap and black mask set against a white face, chin, breast and belly. Gray wings with 2 yellow wing bars. Chestnut flanks.

Female: similar to male, flanks are duller brown

Juvenile: similar to female, has a lime green head and back, a white eye-ring, bright yellow wing bars, lacks chestnut sides

Nest: cup; female builds; 1 brood per year

Eggs: 3-5; white with brown markings

Incubation: 12-13 days; female incubates

Fledging: 10-12 days; female and male feed young

Migration: complete, to Central America

Food: insects, berries

Compare: Shares the yellow cap with Yellow-rumped Warbler (pg. 174), but lacks yellow sides and rump. The Yellow Warbler (pg. 256) is nearly all yellow and lacks Chestnut-sided's white chest and chestnut flanks.

Stan's Notes: Prefers an open, young aspen forest. Often attracted to backyard water gardens during spring and fall migrations. Look for this attractive warbler in spring, hopping high in the branches while it hunts for insects. You will usually only get a glimpse of this fast-moving warbler. Will hold tail in an uplifted position, showing its white undertail. Not uncommon for it to approach humans in defense of a nest site.

Brown Creeper
Certhia americana

YEAR-ROUND
WINTER

Size: 5" (13 cm)

Male: Small, thin, nearly camouflaged brown bird. White from chin to belly. White eyebrows. Long stiff tail. Dark eyes. Thin curved bill.

Female: same as male

Juvenile: same as adult

Nest: cup; female builds; unknown how many broods per year

Eggs: 5-6; white with tiny brown markings

Incubation: 14-17 days; female incubates, male feeds female during incubation

Fledging: 13-16 days; female and male feed young

Migration: partial migrator

Food: insects, nuts, seeds

Compare: Creeps up tree trunks, not down, like the White-breasted Nuthatch (pg. 178). Watch for Creeper to fly from the top of one trunk to the bottom of another, working its way to the top, looking for insects. Slightly larger than the Red-breasted Nuthatch (pg. 170), with a similar white stripe above eyes, but Creeper has a white belly, long tail and lacks a black crown.

Stan's Notes: This bird utilizes its camouflage coloring to defend itself, spreading out flat on a branch or tree trunk without moving. Young are able to follow their parents, creeping soon after fledging. Commonly found in wooded areas. Often builds nest behind loose bark of dead or dying trees.

Chimney Swift
Chaetura pelagica

Size: 5" (13 cm)

Male: Nondescript, swallow-shaped bird, usually seen only in flight. Long, thin brown body with a pointed tail and head. Long swept-back wings are longer than body.

Female: same as male

Juvenile: same as adult

Nest: half cup; female and male build; 1 brood per year

Eggs: 4-5; white without markings

Incubation: 19-21 days; female and male incubate

Fledging: 28-30 days; female and male feed young

Migration: complete, to South America

Food: insects caught in air

Compare: Considerably smaller than Purple Martin (pg. 60) and lacks the iridescent purple of the Martin. The Barn Swallow (pg. 56) has a forked tail unlike the pointed tail of Swift. Tree Swallow (pg. 52) has a white belly and blue green back.

Stan's Notes: One of the fastest fliers in the bird world. Spends all day flying, rarely perching. Bathes and drinks by skimming across water surfaces. Unique in-flight twittering call is often heard before bird is seen. Flies in groups, feeding on flying insects nearly 100 feet (30 m) in the air. Often called Flying Cigar due to its pointed body shape. Hundreds will nest and roost in large chimneys, hence the common name. Builds nest with tiny twigs, cementing it with saliva, attaching it to the inside of a chimney or hollow tree.

Chipping Sparrow
Spizella passerina

SUMMER

Size: 5" (13 cm)

Male: Small gray brown sparrow with a clear gray breast, rusty crown and white eyebrows. A black eye line and thin gray black bill. Two faint wing bars.

Female: same as male

Juvenile: similar to adult, has a streaked breast, lacks the rusty crown

Nest: cup; female builds; 2 broods per year

Eggs: 3-5; blue green with brown markings

Incubation: 11-14 days; female incubates

Fledging: 10-12 days; female and male feed young

Migration: complete, to southern states, Mexico and Central America

Food: insects, seeds; will come to ground feeders

Compare: Similar to American Tree Sparrow (pg. 90), which shares a rust crown, but lacks a dark eye line. The rusty Fox Sparrow (pg. 98) lacks a clear breast. Song Sparrow (pg. 82) has a heavily streaked breast. Female House Finch (pg. 76) also has a streaked breast.

Stan's Notes: A common garden or yard bird, often seen feeding on dropped seeds beneath feeders. Gathers in large family groups to feed in preparation for migration. Migrates at night in flocks of 20-30 birds. The common name comes from the male's fast "chip" call. Often is just called Chippy. Nest is placed low in dense shrubs and is almost always lined with animal hair. Can be very unafraid of people, allowing you to approach closely before it flies away.

male

female

Common Redpoll
Carduelis flammea

WINTER

Size: 5" (13 cm)

Male: A small sparrow-like bird with a bright red crown and black spot on the chin. Heavily streaked back and a splash of raspberry red on the chest.

Female: same as male, but lacking raspberry red on the chest

Juvenile: browner than adults, lacks a red crown, has dark streaks on the chest

Nest: cup; female builds; 1 brood (sometimes 2) per year

Eggs: 4-5; pale green with purple markings

Incubation: 10-11 days; female incubates

Fledging: 11-12 days; female and male feed young

Migration: irruptive; moves into the state from Canada in some winters

Food: seeds, insects; will come to seed feeders

Compare: Slightly smaller than the male Purple Finch (pg. 228), lacking male Purple Finch's red back and rump. Similar to the male House Finch (pg. 226), but lacks the orange red rump. Look for the bright red crown and black spot under the bill.

Stan's Notes: Name is derived from the color and "taking a poll" or counting heads. This bird winters in Wisconsin after summering in the far reaches of Canada. Winter flocks of up to 100 birds are not uncommon. Bathes in snow or open water in winter. Much like the Black-capped Chickadee, it can be tamed and hand fed.

male
pg. 226

female

YEAR-ROUND

House Finch
Carpodacus mexicanus

Size: 5" (13 cm)

Female: A plain brown bird with a heavily streaked white chest.

Male: orange red face, chest and rump, a brown cap, brown marking behind eyes, brown wings streaked with white, streaked belly

Juvenile: similar to female

Nest: cup, sometimes in cavities; female builds; 2 broods per year

Eggs: 4-5; pale blue, lightly marked

Incubation: 12-14 days; female incubates

Fledging: 15-19 days; female and male feed young

Migration: non-migrator to partial migrator; will move around to find food

Food: seeds, fruit, leaf buds; will visit seed feeders

Compare: The female Purple Finch (pg. 88) is very similar, but has bold white eyebrows. The female American Goldfinch (pg. 252) has a clear chest and white wing bars. Similar to Pine Siskin (pg. 80), but lacks yellow wing bars and has a much larger bill than Siskin.

Stan's Notes: Very social bird. Visits feeders in small flocks. Likes nesting in hanging flower baskets. Incubating female is fed by the male. Has a loud, cheerful warbling song. House Finches that were originally introduced to Long Island, New York, from the western U.S. in the 1940s have since populated the entire eastern U.S. Now found across the country. Can be the most common bird at feeders. Suffers from a fatal eye disease that causes the eyes to crust over.

CD 1, TRACK 38

House Wren
Troglodytes aedon

SUMMER

Size: 5" (13 cm)

Male: A small all-brown bird with lighter brown markings on tail and wings. Slightly curved brown bill. Often holds its tail erect.

Female: same as male

Juvenile: same as adult

Nest: cavity; female and male line just about any nest cavity; 2 broods per year

Eggs: 4-6; tan with brown markings

Incubation: 10-13 days; female and male incubate

Fledging: 12-15 days; female and male feed young

Migration: complete, to southern states and Mexico

Food: insects

Compare: Wren's long curved bill and long upturned tail differentiates it from sparrows. Lack of eyebrows distinguishes it from other wrens.

Stan's Notes: A prolific songster, it will sing from dawn until dusk during the mating season. Easily attracted to nest boxes. In spring, the male chooses several prospective nesting cavities and places a few small twigs in each. Female inspects each, chooses one, and finishes the nest building. She will completely fill the nest cavity with uniformly small twigs, then line a small depression at back of cavity with pine needles and grass. Often has trouble fitting long twigs through nest cavity hole. Tries many different directions and approaches until successful.

Pine Siskin
Carduelis pinus

Size: 5" (13 cm)

Male: Small brown finch. Heavily streaked back, breast and belly. Yellow wing bars. Yellow at base of tail. Thin bill.

Female: similar to male, with less yellow

Juvenile: similar to adult, light yellow tinge over the breast and chin

Nest: modified cup; female constructs; 2 broods per year

Eggs: 3-4; greenish blue with brown markings

Incubation: 12-13 days; female incubates

Fledging: 14-15 days; female and male feed young

Migration: irruptive; moves around the United States in search of food

Food: seeds, insects; will come to seed feeders

Compare: Female American Goldfinch (pg. 252) lacks streaks and has white wing bars. Female House Finch (pg. 76) has a streaked chest, but lacks yellow wing bars. Female Purple Finch (pg. 88) has bold white eyebrows.

Stan's Notes: Usually considered a winter finch, found year-round in northern Wisconsin. Common in the southern part of the state in some winters, scarce in others. During invasion years it is more numerous in southern Wisconsin. Comes to thistle feeders. Travels and breeds in small groups. Male feeds female during incubation. Juveniles lose the yellow tint by late summer of the first year. Builds its nest toward the ends of coniferous branches, where needles are dense, helping to conceal. Nests are often only a few feet apart.

CD 1, TRACK 40

SUMMER

Song Sparrow
Melospiza melodia

Size: 5-6" (13-15 cm)

Male: Common brown sparrow with heavy dark streaks on breast coalescing into a central dark spot.

Female: same as male

Juvenile: similar to adult, finely streaked breast, lacks a central spot

Nest: cup; female builds; 2 broods per year

Eggs: 3-4; pale blue to green with reddish brown markings

Incubation: 12-14 days; female incubates

Fledging: 9-12 days; female and male feed young

Migration: complete, to southern states

Food: insects, seeds; rarely visits seed feeders

Compare: Similar to other brown sparrows. Look for a heavily streaked chest with central dark spot.

Stan's Notes: Many Song Sparrow subspecies or varieties, but dark central spot carries through each variant. While the female builds another nest for a second brood, the male sparrow often takes over feeding the young. Returns to a similar area each year, defending a small territory by singing from thick shrubs. A common host of the Brown-headed Cowbird. Ground feeders, look for them to scratch simultaneously with both feet to expose seeds. Unlike many other sparrow species, Song Sparrows rarely flock together. A constant songster, repeating its loud, clear song every couple minutes. Song varies in structure, but is basically the same from region to region.

male pg. 176

female

Dark-eyed Junco

Junco hyemalis

YEAR-ROUND
WINTER

Size: 5½" (14 cm)

Female: A round, dark-eyed bird with tan-to-brown chest, head and back. White belly. Ivory-to-pink bill. Since the outermost tail feathers are white, tail appears as a white V in flight.

Male: same as female, only slate gray to charcoal

Juvenile: similar to female, but has a streaked breast and head

Nest: cup; female and male construct; 2 broods per year

Eggs: 3-5; white with reddish brown markings

Incubation: 12-13 days; female incubates

Fledging: 10-13 days; male and female feed young

Migration: complete, throughout the U.S.

Food: seeds, insects; will come to seed feeders

Compare: Rarely confused with any other bird. Small flocks feed under bird feeders in winter.

Stan's Notes: One of Wisconsin's most common winter residents. Migrates from Canada to Wisconsin and beyond. The females tend to migrate farther south than the males. Adheres to a rigid social hierarchy, with dominant birds chasing less dominant birds. Look for its white outer tail feathers flashing when in flight. Usually seen in small flocks on the ground, where it will "double-scratch" with both feet simultaneously to expose seeds and insects. Consumes many weed seeds. Nests in a wide variety of wooded habitats. Several junco species have now been combined into one, simply called Dark-eyed Junco.

female

male pg. 54

Indigo Bunting

Passerina cyanea

SUMMER

Size: 5½" (14 cm)

Female: Light brown finch-like bird. Faint streaking on a light tan chest. Wings have a very faint blue cast with indistinct wing bars.

Male: vibrant blue finch-like bird, scattered dark markings on wings and tail

Juvenile: similar to female

Nest: cup; female builds; 2 broods per year

Eggs: 3-4; pale blue without markings

Incubation: 12-13 days; female incubates

Fledging: 10-11 days; female feeds young

Migration: complete, to southern Florida, Mexico and Central and South America

Food: insects, seeds, fruit; will visit seed feeders

Compare: Similar to female finches. Female American Goldfinch (pg. 252) has white wing bars. The female Purple Finch (pg. 88) has white eyebrows and a heavily streaked chest. The female House Finch (pg. 76) also has a heavily streaked chest.

Stan's Notes: A secretive bird, usually only the male buntings are seen. Males often sing from treetops to attract mates. Will come to feeders in the spring before insects are plentiful. Mostly seen along woodland edges, feeding on insects. Migrates during the night in flocks of 5-10 birds. A late migrant, males return before the females and juveniles. Juveniles move to within a mile from birth site.

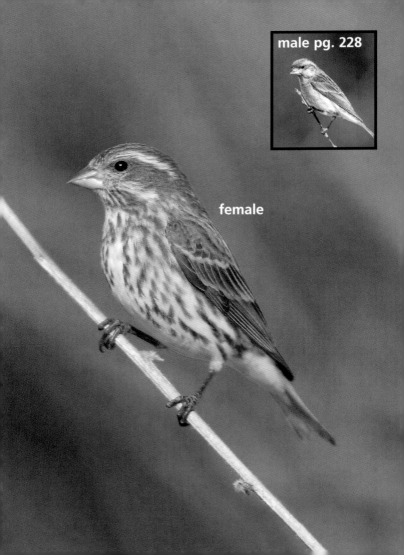

male pg. 228

female

Purple Finch
Carpodacus purpureus

YEAR-ROUND
WINTER

Size: 6" (15 cm)

Female: A plain brown bird with a heavily streaked chest. Prominent white eyebrows.

Male: raspberry red head, cap, breast, back and rump, brownish wings and tail

Juvenile: same as female

Nest: cup; female and male build; 1 brood a year

Eggs: 4-5; greenish blue with brown markings

Incubation: 12-13 days; female incubates

Fledging: 13-14 days; female and male feed young

Migration: irruptive; moves around the state in search of food

Food: seeds, insects, fruit; comes to seed feeders

Compare: Female House Finch (pg. 76) lacks female Purple Finch's white eyebrows. Pine Siskin (pg. 80) has yellow wing bars and a much smaller bill than Purple Finch. The female American Goldfinch (pg. 252) has a clear chest and white wing bars.

Stan's Notes: A year-round finch in the northern half of the state and winter resident in the southern half. Its residency in Wisconsin is long-term, unlike the recent invasion of the House Finch. Visits seed feeders along with House Finches, making it hard to tell them apart. Feeds mainly on seeds, with ash tree seeds a very important food source. Prefers open woods or woodland edges. Travels in flocks of up to 50. Has a rich loud song, with a distinctive "tic" note made only during flight. Not a purple color, the Latin species name *purpureus* means "crimson" or other reddish color.

side view

front view

WINTER

American Tree Sparrow
Spizella arborea

Size: 6" (15 cm)

Male: A common brown sparrow with tan breast and rusty crown. Black spot in the center of breast. Upper bill is dark, lower bill yellow. Two white wing bars. Gray eyebrows.

Female: same as male

Juvenile: lacks a rust crown, has a streaked chest that often obscures the central dark spot

Nest: cup; female builds; 1 brood per year

Eggs: 3-5; green white with brown markings

Incubation: 12-13 days; female incubates

Fledging: 8-10 days; female and male feed young

Migration: complete, to Wisconsin from Canada

Food: insects, seeds; visits seed feeders

Compare: Appears similar to other sparrows, so look closely at the center of the breast for the single dark spot. Shares a rusty crown with the Chipping Sparrow (pg. 72), but lacks Chippy's distinctive white eyebrows and black eye line. Song Sparrow (pg. 82) has a heavily streaked chest.

Stan's Notes: Seen mostly during migration in flocks ranging from 2-200. A regular winter bird feeder visitor throughout Wisconsin. Occasionally called Winter Chippy because it looks similar to the Chipping Sparrow, a summer visitor. Nests in northern Canada and Alaska.

male

female

House Sparrow
Passer domesticus

YEAR-ROUND

Size: 6" (15 cm)

Male: Medium sparrow-like bird with large black spot on throat extending down to the chest. Brown back and single white wing bars. A gray belly and crown.

Female: slightly smaller than the male, light brown, lacks the throat patch and single wing bars

Juvenile: similar to female

Nest: domed cup nest, within cavity; female and male build; 2-3 broods per year

Eggs: 4-6; white with brown markings

Incubation: 10-12 days; female incubates

Fledging: 14-17 days; female and male feed young

Migration: non-migrator; moves around to find food

Food: seeds, insects, fruit; comes to seed feeders

Compare: Lacks the rusty crown of the American Tree Sparrow (pg. 90) and Chipping Sparrow (pg. 72). Harris's Sparrow (pg. 102) has a black "hood" and white chest. Look for the black bib of male and clear chest of female.

Stan's Notes: One of the first bird songs heard in cities in spring. Familiar city bird, nearly always in small flocks. Introduced from Europe to Central Park, New York, in 1850. Now found throughout North America. These birds are not really sparrows, but members of the Weaver Finch family, characterized by their large, oversized domed nests. Constructs a nest containing scraps of plastic, paper and whatever else is available. An aggressive bird that will kill the young of other birds in order to take over a cavity.

CD 1, TRACK 45

white-striped

tan-striped

White-throated Sparrow
Zonotrichia albicollis

MIGRATION
SUMMER
WINTER

Size: 6-7" (15-18 cm)

Male: A brown bird with gray tan chest and belly. Small yellow spot between the eyes (lore). Distinctive white or tan throat patch. White or tan stripes alternate with black stripes on crown. Color of the throat patch and crown stripes match.

Female: same as male

Juvenile: similar to adult, gray throat and eyebrows with heavily streaked chest

Nest: cup; female builds; 1 brood per year

Eggs: 4-6; color varies from greenish to bluish to creamy white with red brown markings

Incubation: 11-14 days; female incubates

Fledging: 10-12 days; female and male feed young

Migration: complete, to southern states and Mexico

Food: insects, seeds, fruit; visits ground feeders

Compare: The White-crowned Sparrow (pg. 96) lacks the throat patch and yellow lore. The Song Sparrow (pg. 82) has a central spot on the chest and lacks the striped pattern on head.

Stan's Notes: There are two color variations (polymorphic): white-striped or tan-striped. Studies have indicated that the white-striped adults tend to mate with the tan-striped birds. No indication why. Nests are built on the ground underneath small trees in bogs and coniferous forests.

juvenile

White-crowned Sparrow
Zonotrichia leucophrys

MIGRATION
WINTER

Size: 6½-7½" (16-19 cm)

Male: A brown sparrow with a gray breast and a black-and-white striped crown. Small, thin pink bill.

Female: same as male

Juvenile: similar to adult, with brown stripes on the head instead of white

Nest: cup; female builds; 2 broods per year

Eggs: 3-5; color varies from greenish to bluish to whitish with red brown markings

Incubation: 11-14 days; female incubates

Fledging: 8-12 days; male and female feed young

Migration: complete, to southern Wisconsin, southern states and Mexico

Food: insects, seeds, berries; visits ground feeders

Compare: The White-throated Sparrow (pg. 94) has a white or tan throat patch, and yellow spot between eyes and bill, with a blackish bill.

Stan's Notes: Usually seen in groups of up to 20 during migration, when it can be seen feeding beneath seed feeders. A ground feeder, scratching backward with both feet at the same time. Males arrive before females and establish territories by singing from perches. Male takes most of the responsibility of raising young while female starts the second brood. Only 9-12 days separate broods. Nests in Canada and Alaska.

Fox Sparrow

Passerella iliaca

MIGRATION
WINTER

Size: 7" (18 cm)

Male: A plump rusty red sparrow with a heavily streaked, rust-colored breast and solid rust tail. Head and back are mottled with gray.

Female: same as male

Juvenile: same as adult

Nest: cup; female builds; 2 broods per year

Eggs: 2-4; pale green with reddish markings

Incubation: 12-14 days; female incubates

Fledging: 10-11 days; female and male feed young

Migration: complete, to southern Wisconsin, southern states

Food: insects, seeds; comes to feeders

Compare: Similar coloration as the Brown Thrasher (pg. 122), but the Fox Sparrow is smaller, plumper and has a smaller bill. Rusty color differentiates it from all other sparrows.

Stan's Notes: One of the largest sparrows. Often seen only under seed feeders during migration. Usually alone or in small groups looking for seeds and insects underneath feeders. Scratches like a chicken with both feet at the same time to find food. The common name "Sparrow" comes from the Anglo-Saxon word *spearwa*, meaning "flutterer," as applied to any small bird. "Fox" refers to the bird's rusty color. Nests on the ground in brush and along forest edges in Canada.

male
pg. 2

female

SUMMER

Eastern Towhee
Pipilo erythrophthalmus

Size: 7-8" (18-20 cm)

Female: A mostly light brown bird. Rusty red brown sides and white belly. Long brown tail with white tip. Short, stout, pointed bill and rich red eyes. White wing patches flash in flight.

Male: similar to female, but is black, not brown

Juvenile: light brown, a heavily streaked head, chest and belly, long dark tail with white tip

Nest: cup; female builds; 2 broods per year

Eggs: 3-4; creamy white with brown markings

Incubation: 12-13 days; female incubates

Fledging: 10-12 days; male and female feed young

Migration: complete, to southern states, Mexico and Central and South America

Food: insects, seeds, fruit; visits ground feeders

Compare: Slightly smaller than the American Robin (pg. 190).

Stan's Notes: Common name comes from its distinctive "tow-hee" call given by both sexes. Mostly known for its characteristic call that sounds like, "Drink-your-tea!" Seen hopping backward with both feet (bilateral scratching), raking up leaf litter in search of insects and seeds. The female broods, but the male does the most feeding of young. In southern coastal states, some have red eyes and others have white eyes.

juvenile

Harris's Sparrow
Zonotrichia querula

MIGRATION

Size: 7½" (19 cm)

Male: A very large sparrow with various amounts of black on head, extending down the nape and face onto the chest. White belly. Brown back and wings. Pink bill and legs.

Female: same as male

Juvenile: similar to adult, lacks the black "hood" and spotted chest

Nest: cup, on the ground; unknown who builds; 1 brood per year

Eggs: 4-5; white with brown markings

Incubation: 13-14 days; female incubates

Fledging: 11-12 days; female and male feed young

Migration: complete, to southern states

Food: insects, seeds, berries; visits ground feeders

Compare: The House Sparrow (pg. 92) lacks the black "hood" of Harris's Sparrow.

Stan's Notes: A large sparrow commonly seen in small groups of up to ten birds, scratching beneath seed feeders during migration. Nests in northern Canada, returning to the central U.S. for winter. Recent studies show that a bird's status is dependent upon the amount of black on its "hood," not its age. The more black, the higher the status. Was named after Edward Harris (1799-1863), a companion of John James Audubon.

1 year old

Bohemian
Waxwing

YEAR-ROUND

Cedar Waxwing
Bombycilla cedrorum

Size: 7½" (19 cm)

Male: Very sleek-looking gray-to-brown bird with pointed crest, light yellow belly and bandit-like black mask. Tip of tail is bright yellow and the tips of wings look as if they have been dipped in red wax.

Female: same as male

Juvenile: grayish with a heavily streaked chest, lacks red wing tips, black mask and sleek look

Nest: cup; female and male construct; 1 brood per year, occasionally 2

Eggs: 4-6; pale blue with brown markings

Incubation: 10-12 days; female incubates

Fledging: 14-18 days; female and male feed young

Migration: partial migrator; moves around to find food

Food: cedar cones, fruit, insects

Compare: Similar to its larger, less common cousin, Bohemian Waxwing (see inset), which has white on wings and rust under tail. Female Cardinal (pg. 114) has a large red bill.

Stan's Notes: The name is derived from its red wax-like wing tips and preference for eating small blueberry-like cones of the cedar. Mostly seen in flocks, moving from area to area, looking for berries. Wanders in winter to find available food supplies. During summer, before berries are abundant, it feeds on insects. Spends most of its time at the tops of tall trees. Listen for the very high-pitched "sreee" whistling sounds it constantly makes. Obtains mask after first year and red wing tips after second year.

CD 1, TRACK 50

male pg. 4

female

SUMMER

Brown-headed Cowbird
Molothrus ater

Size: 7½" (19 cm)

Female: Dull brown bird with no obvious markings. Pointed, sharp gray bill.

Male: glossy black bird, chocolate brown head

Juvenile: similar to female, only dull gray color and a streaked chest

Nest: no nest; lays eggs in nests of other birds

Eggs: 5-7; white with brown markings

Incubation: 10-13 days; host bird incubates eggs

Fledging: 10-11 days; host birds feed young

Migration: complete, to southern states

Food: insects, seeds; will come to seed feeders

Compare: Female Red-winged Blackbird (pg. 116) is slightly larger and has white eyebrows and a streaked chest. European Starling (pg. 6) has speckles and a shorter tail.

Stan's Notes: A member of the blackbird family. Of approximately 750 species of parasitic birds worldwide, this is the only parasitic bird in the state, laying eggs in host birds' nests, leaving others to raise its young. Cowbirds are known to have laid eggs in nests of over 200 species of birds. Some birds reject cowbird eggs, but most incubate them and raise the young, even to the exclusion of their own. Look for warblers and other birds feeding young birds twice their own size. At one time cowbirds followed bison to feed on insects attracted to the animals.

Horned Lark
Eremophila alpestris

SUMMER

Size: 7-8" (18-20 cm)

Male: A sleek tan-to-brown bird. Black necklace with a yellow chin and black bill. Two tiny "horns" on the top of head can be difficult to see. A dark tail with white outer feathers, noticeable in flight.

Female: duller than male, "horns" less noticeable

Juvenile: lacks the black markings and yellow chin, doesn't form "horns" until second year

Nest: ground; female builds; 2-3 broods per year

Eggs: 3-4; gray with brown markings

Incubation: 11-12 days; female incubates

Fledging: 9-12 days; female and male feed young

Migration: complete, to southern states

Food: seeds, insects

Compare: Smaller than Meadowlark (pg. 266), which shares the black necklace and yellow chin. Look for the black marks in front of eyes.

Stan's Notes: The only true lark native to North America. One of the earliest migrators, moving into Wisconsin in February. Horned Larks are birds of open ground. Common in rural areas, frequently seen in large flocks. Population increased in North America over the past 100 years due to land clearing for farming. May have up to three broods per year because they get such an early start. The male performs a fluttering courtship flight high in the air while singing a high-pitched song. Female performs a distraction display if nest is disturbed. Can renest about a week after brood fledges. The name "Lark" comes from the Middle English word *laverock*, or "a lark."

female

male pg. 28

Rose-breasted Grosbeak
Pheucticus ludovicianus

SUMMER

Size: 7-8" (18-20 cm)

Female: Plump, heavily streaked brown and white bird with obvious white eyebrows. Orange yellow wing linings.

Male: black-and-white bird with large, triangular rose patch in center of chest, wing linings rosy red

Juvenile: similar to female

Nest: cup; female and male construct; 1-2 broods per year

Eggs: 3-5; blue green with brown markings

Incubation: 13-14 days; female and male incubate

Fledging: 9-12 days; female and male feed young

Migration: complete, to Mexico, Central America and South America

Food: insects, seeds, fruit; comes to seed feeders

Compare: Looks like a large sparrow. Larger and has a more distinctive eyebrow mark than female Purple Finch (pg. 88). Female House Finch (pg. 76) lacks the eyebrow mark.

Stan's Notes: Often prefers mature deciduous forest for nesting. Both sexes sing, but the male sings much louder and clearer. Has a rich, robin-like song. "Grosbeak" refers to its large bill, used to crush seeds. Late to arrive in spring; early to leave in fall. Males arrive in small groups first, joined by females several days later. Several males can be seen visiting seed feeders at the same time in spring. When females arrive, males become territorial and reduce their visits to feeders. Young grosbeaks visit feeders with adults after fledging.

winter

breeding

SUMMER

Spotted Sandpiper
Actitis macularius

Size: 8" (20 cm)

Male: Olive brown back. Long bill and long dull yellow legs. White line over eyes. Breeding plumage has black spots on a white chest and belly. Winter has a clear chest and belly.

Female: same as male

Juvenile: similar to winter adult, with a darker bill

Nest: ground; female and male build; 2 broods per year

Eggs: 3-4; brownish with brown markings

Incubation: 20-24 days; male incubates

Fledging: 17-21 days; male feeds young

Migration: complete, to southern states, Mexico and Central and South America

Food: aquatic insects

Compare: Smaller than Lesser Yellowlegs (pg. 126). The Killdeer (pg. 124) has 2 black bands around neck. Look for Sandpiper to bob its tail up and down while standing. Look for breeding Spotted Sandpiper's black spots extending from chest to belly.

Stan's Notes: One of the few shorebirds that will dive underwater if pursued. Able to fly straight up out of the water. Flies with wings held in a cup-like arc, rarely lifting them above a horizontal plane. Constantly bobs its tail while standing and walks as if delicately balanced. Female mates with multiple males and lays eggs in up to five different nests. Male incubates and cares for young. In winter plumage, it lacks black spots on the chest and belly.

CD 1, TRACK 52

male pg. 234

female

juvenile

YEAR-ROUND

Northern Cardinal
Cardinalis cardinalis

Size: 8-9" (20-22.5 cm)

Female: Buff brown bird with tinges of red on crest and wings, a black mask and large red bill.

Male: red bird with a black mask extending from face down to chin and throat, large red bill and crest

Juvenile: same as female, but with a blackish gray bill

Nest: cup; female builds; 2-3 broods per year

Eggs: 3-4; bluish white with brown markings

Incubation: 12-13 days; female and male incubate

Fledging: 9-10 days; female and male feed young

Migration: non-migrator

Food: seeds, insects, fruit; comes to seed feeders

Compare: The male Red Crossbill (pg. 230) has dark brown wings and a thinner crossed bill. The Cedar Waxwing (pg. 104) has a small dark bill. The female Northern Cardinal appears similar to juvenile Cardinal, but the juvenile has a dark bill. Look for the bright red bill of female Cardinal.

Stan's Notes: A familiar backyard bird. Look for the male feeding female during courtship. Male feeds young of the first brood by himself while female builds second nest. The name comes from the Latin word *cardinalis*, which means "important." Very territorial in spring, it will fight its own reflection in a window. Non-territorial during winter, gathering in small flocks of up to 20 birds. Both the female and male sing and can be heard anytime of year. Listen for its "whata-cheer-cheer-cheer" territorial call in spring.

CD 1, TRACK 53

male pg. 8

female

Red-winged Blackbird
Agelaius phoeniceus

SUMMER

Size: 8½" (22 cm)

Female: Heavily streaked brown bird with a pointed brown bill and white eyebrows.

Male: jet black bird with red and yellow patches on upper wings, pointed black bill

Juvenile: same as female

Nest: cup; female builds; 2-3 broods per year

Eggs: 3-4; bluish green with brown markings

Incubation: 10-12 days; female incubates

Fledging: 11-14 days; female and male feed young

Migration: complete, to southern states, Mexico and Central America

Food: seeds, insects; will come to seed feeders

Compare: Female Brown-headed Cowbird (pg. 106) and Yellow-headed Blackbird (pg. 120) lack the white eyebrows and heavily streaked breast. Similar to the female Rose-breasted Grosbeak (pg. 110), but Red-winged has a thinner body and pointed bill.

Stan's Notes: One of the most widespread and numerous birds in the state. It is a sure sign of spring when the Red-winged Blackbirds return to the marshes. Flocks of up to 100,000 birds have been reported. Males return before the females and defend territories by singing from tops of surrounding vegetation. Males repeat call from the tops of cattails while showing off their red and yellow wing bars (epaulets). Females choose mate and usually will nest over shallow water in thick stands of cattails. Red-wingeds feed mostly on seeds in fall and spring, switching to insects during summer.

female

male

Common Nighthawk
Chordeiles minor

SUMMER

Size: 9" (22.5 cm)

Male: A camouflaged brown and white bird with white chin. A distinctive white band across wings and the tail, seen only in flight.

Female: similar to male, but with tan chin, lacks the white tail band

Juvenile: similar to female

Nest: no nest; lays eggs on the ground, usually on rocks, or on rooftop; 1 brood per year

Eggs: 2; cream with lavender markings

Incubation: 19-20 days; female and male incubate

Fledging: 20-21 days; female and male feed young

Migration: complete, to South America

Food: insects caught in air

Compare: Much larger than Chimney Swift (pg. 70). Look for the obvious white wing band of Nighthawk in flight, and the characteristic flap-flap-flap-glide flight pattern.

Stan's Notes: Usually only seen flying at dusk or after sunset, but not uncommon for it to be sitting on a fence post, sleeping during the day. A very noisy bird, repeating a "peenting" call during flight. Alternates slow wing beats with bursts of quick wing beats. Prolific insect eater. Prefers gravel rooftops for nesting in cities and nests on the ground in country. Male's distinctive springtime mating ritual is a steep diving flight terminated with a loud popping noise. One of the first birds to migrate each autumn.

male pg. 10

female

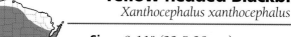

Yellow-headed Blackbird
Xanthocephalus xanthocephalus

SUMMER

Size: 9-11" (22.5-28 cm)

Female: A large brown bird with a dull yellow head and chest. Slightly smaller than male.

Male: black bird with a lemon yellow head, chest and nape of neck, black mask and gray bill, white wing patches

Juvenile: similar to female

Nest: cup; female builds; 2 broods per year

Eggs: 3-5; greenish white with brown markings

Incubation: 11-13 days; female incubates

Fledging: 9-12 days; female feeds young

Migration: complete, to southern states and Mexico

Food: insects, seeds; will come to ground feeders

Compare: Larger than female Red-winged Blackbird (pg. 116), which has white eyebrows and a streaked chest.

Stan's Notes: Usually heard before seen, Yellow-headed Blackbird has a low, hoarse, raspy or metallic call. Nests in deep water marshes unlike its cousin, the Red-winged Blackbird, which prefers shallow water. The male gives an impressive mating display, flying with head drooped and feet and tail pointing down while steadily beating its wings. The female incubates alone and feeds 3-5 young. Young keep low and out of sight for as many as three weeks before starting to fly. Migrates in flocks of up to 200 with other blackbirds. Flocks made up mainly of males return first in April; females return later. Most colonies consist of 20-100 nests.

Brown Thrasher
Toxostoma rufum

SUMMER

Size: 11" (28 cm)

Male: A rusty red bird with long tail and heavily streaked breast and belly. Two white wing bars. Long curved bill. Bright yellow eyes.

Female: same as male

Juvenile: same as adult, but eye color is grayish

Nest: cup; female and male construct; 2 broods per year

Eggs: 4-5; pale blue with brown markings

Incubation: 11-14 days; female and male incubate

Fledging: 10-13 days; female and male feed young

Migration: complete, to southern states

Food: insects, fruit

Compare: Slightly larger in size and similar in shape to the American Robin (pg. 190) and Gray Catbird (pg. 188), but the Thrasher has a streaked chest, rusty color and yellow eyes. Similar rust color as Fox Sparrow (pg. 98), but Brown Thrasher is larger and thinner.

Stan's Notes: A prodigious songster, often in thick shrubs where it sings deliberate musical phrases, repeating each twice. Male has the largest documented song repertoire of all North American birds, with over 1,100 song types. Often seen quickly flying or running in and out of dense shrubs. Noisy feeding due to habit of turning over leaves, small rocks and branches. This bird is more abundant in the central Great Plains than anywhere else in North America.

Killdeer
Charadrius vociferus

SUMMER

Size: 11" (28 cm)

Male: An upland shorebird that has 2 black bands around the neck like a necklace. A brown back and white belly. Bright reddish orange rump, visible in flight.

Female: same as male

Juvenile: similar to adult, with 1 neck band

Nest: ground; male builds; 2 broods per year

Eggs: 3-5; tan with brown markings

Incubation: 24-28 days; male and female incubate

Fledging: 25 days; male and female lead their young to food

Migration: complete, to southern states, Mexico and Central America

Food: insects

Compare: The Spotted Sandpiper (pg. 112) is found around water and lacks the 2 neck bands of the Killdeer.

Stan's Notes: The only shorebird with two black neck bands. It is known for its broken wing impression, which draws intruders away from nest. Once clear of the nest, the Killdeer takes flight. Nests are only a slight depression in a gravel area, often very difficult to see. Young look like miniature adults on stilts when first hatched. Able to follow parents and peck for insects soon after birth. Technically classified as a shorebird, but doesn't live at the shore. Often seen in vacant fields or by railroads. Migrates in small flocks. Gives a very distinctive "kill-deer" call.

Lesser Yellowlegs
Tringa flavipes

MIGRATION

Size: 10-11" (25-28 cm)

Male: A typical sandpiper-type bird with a brown back and wings and lightly streaked white breast and belly. Thin, straight black bill. Long yellow legs.

Female: same as male

Juvenile: same as adult

Nest: ground; female builds; 1 brood per year

Eggs: 3-4; yellowish with brown markings

Incubation: 22-23 days; male and female incubate.

Fledging: 18-20 days; male and female lead young to food

Migration: complete, to southern coastal states, South America

Food: aquatic insects, tiny fish

Compare: Very similar to Greater Yellowlegs (pg. 138), but is smaller with a shorter bill. Breeding Sandpiper (pg. 112) has spots on its chest.

Stan's Notes: Usually seen in small flocks, it combs shorelines and mud flats looking for aquatic insects. Most often seen in the head down, tail up position, walking along, looking to snatch up food. Uses its long straight bill to pluck insects and tiny fish from water. Very shy bird that quite often moves into the water prior to taking flight. Has a variety of "flight" notes that it gives when taking off. A member of the group of sandpipers called Tattlers, all of which scream alarm calls when taking flight. Nests on marshes in spruce forests of central Alaska and central Canada. Migrates later than the Greater Yellowlegs in spring and earlier in fall.

CD 2, TRACK 4

male

female

American Kestrel
Falco sparverius

SUMMER
WINTER

Size: 10-12" (25-30 cm); up to 2-foot wingspan

Male: Rusty brown back and tail. A white breast with dark spots. Double black vertical lines on white face. Blue gray wings. Distinctive wide black band with a white edge on tip of rusty tail.

Female: similar to male, but slightly larger, has rusty brown wings and dark bands on tail

Juvenile: same as adult of the same sex

Nest: cavity; doesn't build a nest within; 1 brood per year

Eggs: 4-5; white with brown markings

Incubation: 29-31 days; male and female incubate

Fledging: 30-31 days; female and male feed young

Migration: complete, to southern states, Mexico and Central America; small percentage will not migrate

Food: insects, small mammals and birds, reptiles

Compare: Similar to other falcons. Look for 2 vertical black stripes on the Kestrel's face. No other small bird of prey has a rusty back and tail.

Stan's Notes: A falcon that was once called Sparrow Hawk due to its small size. Could be called Grasshopper Hawk because it eats many grasshoppers. Hovers close to roads before diving for prey. Adapts quickly to a wooden nesting box. Has pointed swept-back wings, seen in flight. Perches nearly upright. Unusual raptor in that males and females have quite different markings. Watch for them to pump their tails up and down after landing on perches.

male

female

Northern Flicker
Colaptes auratus

SUMMER

Size: 12" (30 cm)

Male: Brown and black woodpecker with a large white rump patch visible only when flying. Black necklace above a speckled breast. Red spot on nape of neck and black mustache.

Female: same as male, but lacking a black mustache

Juvenile: same as adult of the same sex

Nest: cavity; female and male excavate; 1 brood per year

Eggs: 5-8; white without markings

Incubation: 11-14 days; female and male incubate

Fledging: 25-28 days; female and male feed young

Migration: complete, to southern states

Food: insects, especially ants and beetles

Compare: The male Yellow-bellied Sapsucker (pg. 30) is smaller and has a red chin and forehead. The male Red-bellied Woodpecker (pg. 36) has a red crown, a black-and-white zebra-striped back and lacks a mustache. Flickers are the only brown-backed woodpeckers in the state.

Stan's Notes: This is the only woodpecker to regularly feed on the ground. Preferring ants and beetles, it produces an antacid saliva to neutralize the acidic defense of ants. Male usually selects nest site, taking up to 12 days to excavate. Some have had success attracting flickers to nest boxes stuffed with sawdust. In flight, flashes golden yellow under the wings and tail, undulates deeply and gives a loud "wacka-wacka" call.

Mourning Dove
Zenaida macroura

YEAR-ROUND
SUMMER

Size: 12" (30 cm)

Male: Smooth fawn-colored dove with gray patch on the head. Iridescent pink, green around neck. A single black spot behind and below eyes. Black spots on wings and tail. Pointed wedge-shaped tail with white edges.

Female: similar to male, lacking iridescent pink and green neck feathers

Juvenile: spotted and streaked

Nest: platform; female and male build; 2 broods per year

Eggs: 2; white without markings

Incubation: 13-14 days; male and female incubate, the male during day, female at night

Fledging: 12-14 days; female and male feed young

Migration: partial migrator to complete; moves around to find food or migrates to southern states

Food: seeds; will visit seed and ground feeders

Compare: Smaller than Rock Pigeon (pg. 196), lacking its wide range of color combinations.

Stan's Notes: Name comes from its mournful cooing. A ground feeder, bobbing its head as it walks. One of the few birds to drink without lifting its head, same as Rock Pigeon. Parents feed young a regurgitated liquid called crop-milk for the first few days of life. Flimsy platform nest of twigs often falls apart during a storm. Wind rushing through wing feathers during flight creates a characteristic whistling sound.

 CD 2, TRACK 7

winter

breeding

Pied-billed Grebe
Podilymbus podiceps

SUMMER

Size: 13" (33 cm)

Male: Small brown water bird with a black chin and black ring around a thick, chicken-like ivory bill. Puffy white patch under the tail. Has an unmarked brown bill during winter.

Female: same as male

Juvenile: paler than adult, with white spots and gray chest, belly and bill

Nest: floating platform; female and male build; 1 brood per year

Eggs: 5-7; bluish white without markings

Incubation: 22-24 days; female and male incubate

Fledging: 22-24 days; female and male feed young

Migration: complete, to southern states, Mexico and Central America

Food: crayfish, aquatic insects, fish

Compare: Look for a puffy white patch under the tail and thick, chicken-like bill to help identify.

Stan's Notes: Very common in summer, often seen diving for food. Slowly sinks like a submarine if disturbed. Sinks without diving by quickly compressing feathers to force air out. Was called Hell-diver because of the length of time it can stay submerged. Can surface far from where it went under. Very sensitive to pollution. Adapted well to life on water, with short wings, lobed toes, and legs set close to rear of body. While swimming is easy, it is very awkward on land. Builds nest on a floating mat in water. "Grebe" probably came from the Old English *krib*, meaning "crest," a reference to the crested head plumes of many grebes, especially during breeding season.

male pg. 38

female

Bufflehead
Bucephala albeola

MIGRATION
WINTER

Size: 13-15" (33-38 cm)

Female: Brownish gray duck with dark brown head. White patch on cheek, just behind eyes.

Male: striking black and white duck with a head that shines green purple in sunlight, large white bonnet-like patch on back of head

Juvenile: similar to female

Nest: cavity; female lines old woodpecker cavity; 1 brood per year

Eggs: 8-10; ivory to olive without markings

Incubation: 29-31 days; female incubates

Fledging: 50-55 days; female leads young to food

Migration: complete, to the shores of Lake Michigan and the Mississippi River, southern states, Mexico and Central America

Food: aquatic insects

Compare: Commonly confused with female Common Goldeneye (pg. 150), which lacks the white cheek patch.

Stan's Notes: Common diving duck that travels with other ducks. Seen on rivers and lakes. Nests in old woodpecker cavities. Unlike other ducks, the young remain in the nest for up to two days before venturing out with their mother. Female is very territorial and stays with the same mate for many years.

Greater Yellowlegs
Tringa melanoleuca

MIGRATION

Size: 14" (36 cm)

Male: Tall bird with a bulbous head and long thin bill, slightly upturned. Gray streaking on chest. White belly. Long yellow legs.

Female: same as male

Juvenile: same as adult

Nest: ground; female builds; 1 brood per year

Eggs: 3-4; off-white with brown markings

Incubation: 22-23 days; female and male incubate

Fledging: 18-20 days; male and female feed young

Migration: complete, to southern states, Mexico and Central and South America

Food: small fish, aquatic insects

Compare: Nearly a carbon copy of Lesser Yellowlegs (pg. 126), but is larger and has an upturned bill that is longer than the straight bill of the Lesser Yellowlegs.

Stan's Notes: A common shorebird that can be identified by the slightly upturned bill and long yellow legs. Often seen resting on one leg. Its long legs carry it through deep water. Feeds by rushing forward through the water, plowing its bill or swinging it from side to side, catching small fish and insects. A skittish bird quick to give an alarm call, causing flocks to take flight. Quite often moves into the water prior to taking flight. Has a variety of "flight" notes that it gives when taking off. Nests on the ground close to water on the northern tundra of Labrador and Newfoundland.

CD 2, TRACK 9

male

female

Blue-winged Teal
Anas discors

SUMMER

Size: 15-16" (38-40 cm)

Male: Small, plain-looking brown duck speckled with black. A gray head with a large white crescent-shaped mark at base of bill. Black tail with small white patch. Blue wing patch (speculum) usually seen only in flight.

Female: duller version of male, lacks facial crescent mark and white patch on tail, showing only slight white at base of bill

Juvenile: same as female

Nest: ground; female builds; 1 brood per year

Eggs: 8-11; creamy white

Incubation: 23-27 days; female incubates

Fledging: 35-44 days; female feeds young

Migration: complete, to southern states, Mexico and Central America

Food: aquatic plants, seeds, aquatic insects

Compare: Male Blue-winged has a distinct white face marking. Female Wood Duck (pg. 148) and Mallard (pg. 156) are larger than the female Teal, and Wood Duck has a crest.

Stan's Notes: This is one of the smallest ducks in North America. Common breeding duck in Wisconsin. Builds nest some distance from water. Female performs a distraction display to protect nest and young. Male leaves female near end of incubation. Widespread nesting, breeding as far north as Alaska. One of the longest distance migrating ducks. Planting crops and cultivating to pond edges have caused a decline in population.

CD 2, TRACK 10

soaring

Broad-winged Hawk
Buteo platypterus

MIGRATION
SUMMER

Size: 14-19" (36-48 cm); up to 3-foot wingspan

Male: A hawk slightly smaller than the American Crow, the Broad-winged has a brown back and rusty red barring on chest. Tail has 2-3 wide black-and-white bands. White under wings with black "fingertips," seen in flight.

Female: same as male

Juvenile: tail bands narrower and more numerous, a brown-streaked chest and belly

Nest: platform; female and male build, but female finishes; 1 brood per year

Eggs: 2-3; off-white with brown markings

Incubation: 28-32 days; female incubates, male feeds female during incubation

Fledging: 34-35 days; female and male feed young

Migration: complete, to Central and South America

Food: small mammals, small birds, large insects, snakes, frogs

Compare: Similar in size to Cooper's Hawk (pg. 200), but with a wider, shorter tail. Larger than Sharp-shinned Hawk (pg. 198). Look for the alternating black-and-white tail bands.

Stan's Notes: A very common woodland hawk in the state. Often seen in large groups (kettles) migrating early in autumn. Massive migration provides a spectacular sight along the Great Lakes shoreline. Spends most of its time hunting small birds, snakes and frogs in dense woodlands. Short round wings propel it through dense woods. Screams "call" repetitively when intruders are near the nest.

drumming

Ruffed Grouse
Bonasa umbellus

YEAR-ROUND

Size: 16-19" (40-48 cm); up to 2-foot wingspan

Male: Brown chicken-like bird with long squared tail. Wide black band near tip of tail. Is able to fan tail like a turkey. Tuft of feathers on the head stands like a crown. Black ruffs on sides of neck.

Female: same as male, but less obvious neck ruffs

Juvenile: same as female

Nest: ground; female builds; 1 brood per year

Eggs: 9-12; tan with light brown markings

Incubation: 23-24 days; female incubates

Fledging: 10-12 days; female leads young to food

Migration: non-migrator

Food: seeds, insects, fruit, leaf buds

Compare: Female Ring-necked Pheasant (pg. 158) is larger with a longer, pointed tail. Look for a feathered tuft on the head and black ruffs on the neck of the Ruffed Grouse.

Stan's Notes: A common bird of deep woods. Often seen in aspen or other trees, feeding on leaf buds. In the more northern climates, grows bristles on its feet during the winter to serve as snowshoes. When there is enough snow, it will dive into a snowbank to roost at night. In spring, male raises crest (tuft), fans tail feathers, and stands on logs and drums with wings to attract females. Drumming sound comes from cupped wings moving the air, not pounding on its chest or a log. Female will perform distraction display to protect young. Two color morphs, red and gray, most apparent in the tail. Black ruffs around the neck gave rise to its common name.

male pg. 40

female

Hooded Merganser
Lophodytes cucullatus

MIGRATION
SUMMER
WINTER

Size: 16-19" (40-48 cm)

Female: Sleek brown and rust bird with a red head. Ragged "hair" on back of head. Long, thin brown bill.

Male: same size and shape as female, but a black back and rust sides, crest "hood" raises to reveal large white patch, long black bill

Juvenile: similar to female

Nest: cavity; female lines old woodpecker hole; 1 brood per year

Eggs: 10-12; white without markings

Incubation: 32-33 days; female incubates

Fledging: 71 days; female feeds young

Migration: complete, to southern states

Food: small fish, aquatic insects

Compare: Smaller than female Common Merganser (pg. 238), which has a white chin and large orange bill.

Stan's Notes: A small diving bird of shallow ponds, sloughs, lakes and rivers. Male Hooded Merganser can voluntarily raise and lower its crest to show off the large white head patch. Rarely found away from wooded areas, where it nests in natural cavities or nest boxes. Female will "dump" her eggs into other female Hooded Merganser nests, resulting in 20-25 eggs in some nests. Known to share nest cavities with Common Goldeneyes and Wood Ducks, sitting side by side. Not as common as the Common Merganser.

female

male pg. 214

Wood Duck
Aix sponsa

SUMMER

Size: 17-20" (43-50 cm)

Female: A small brown dabbling duck. Bright white eye-ring and a not-so-obvious crest. A blue patch on wing is often hidden.

Male: highly ornamented with a green head and crest patterned with white and black, rusty chest, white belly and red eyes

Juvenile: same as female

Nest: cavity; female lines old woodpecker cavity; 1 brood per year

Eggs: 10-15; creamy white without markings

Incubation: 28-36 days; female incubates

Fledging: 56-68 days; female teaches young to feed

Migration: complete, to southern states

Food: aquatic insects, plants, seeds

Compare: Female Mallard (pg. 156) and female Blue-winged Teal (pg. 140) lack the bright white eye-ring and crest. The female Northern Shoveler (pg. 152) is larger and has a large spoon-shaped bill.

Stan's Notes: A common duck of quiet, shallow backwater ponds. Nests in old woodpecker holes or in nest boxes. Often seen flying deep in forests or perched high on tree branches. Female takes to flight with a loud squealing call, entering nest cavity from full flight. Will lay eggs in a neighboring female nest (egg dumping), resulting in some clutches in excess of 20 eggs. Young stay in nest cavity only 24 hours after hatching, then jump from up to 30 feet (9 m) to the ground or water to follow their mother, never returning to the nest.

female

male pg. 44

MIGRATION
SUMMER
WINTER

Common Goldeneye
Bucephala clangula

Size: 18½-20" (47-50 cm)

Female: A brown and gray duck with a large dark brown head and gray body. White collar. Bright golden eyes. Yellow-tipped dark bill.

Male: mostly white duck with a black back and a large, puffy green head, large white spot in front of each bright golden eye, dark bill

Juvenile: same as female, but has a dark bill

Nest: cavity; female lines old woodpecker cavity; 1 brood per year

Eggs: 8-10; light green without markings

Incubation: 28-32 days; female incubates

Fledging: 56-59 days; female leads young to food

Migration: complete, to southwestern Wisconsin along the Mississippi River, southern states and Mexico

Food: aquatic plants, insects

Compare: Female Bufflehead (pg. 136) is similar, but smaller and has a white patch on the cheek. Look for the Goldeneye's dark brown head and white collar.

Stan's Notes: Known for its loud whistling, produced by its wings in flight. In late winter and early spring, male often attracts female through elaborate displays, throwing its head backward while it utters a single raspy note. Female will lay eggs in other goldeneye nests, which results in some mothers incubating up to 30 eggs. Received the common name from its obvious bright golden eyes.

male pg. 216

female

Northern Shoveler
Anas clypeata

MIGRATION
SUMMER

Size: 20" (50 cm)

Female: Medium-sized brown duck speckled with black. Green speculum. An extraordinarily large spoon-shaped bill, almost always held pointed toward the water.

Male: iridescent green head, rusty sides and white breast, spoon-shaped bill

Juvenile: same as female

Nest: ground; female builds; 1 brood per year

Eggs: 9-12; olive without markings

Incubation: 22-25 days; female incubates

Fledging: 30-60 days; female leads young to food

Migration: complete, to southern states, Mexico and Central America

Food: aquatic insects, plants

Compare: Similar color as female Mallard (pg. 156), but Mallard lacks the Shoveler's large bill. Female Wood Duck (pg. 148) is smaller and has a white eye-ring. Look for the Shoveler's large spoon-shaped bill to help identify.

Stan's Notes: One of several species of shoveler, so called because of the peculiar shape of its bill. The Northern Shoveler is the only species of these ducks in North America. Found in small flocks of 5-10, swimming low in water with its large bill pointed toward the water, as if it's too heavy to lift. Feeds mainly by filtering tiny aquatic insects and plants from the water's surface with its bill.

YEAR-ROUND

Barred Owl
Strix varia

Size: 20-24" (50-60 cm); up to 3½-foot wingspan

Male: A chunky brown and gray owl with a large head and dark brown eyes. Dark horizontal barring on upper chest. Vertical streaks on lower chest and belly. Yellow bill and feet.

Female: same as male, only slightly larger

Juvenile: light gray with a black face

Nest: cavity; does not add any nesting material; 1 brood per year

Eggs: 2-3; white without markings

Incubation: 28-33 days; female incubates

Fledging: 42-44 days; female and male feed young

Migration: non-migrator

Food: mammals, birds, fish, reptiles, amphibians

Compare: Lacks the "horns" of the Great Horned Owl (pg. 164) and ear tufts of the tiny Eastern Screech-Owl (pg. 192). Eastern Screech-Owl is less than half the size of Barred Owl.

Stan's Notes: A very common owl that can often be seen hunting during the day, perching and watching for mice, birds and other prey. One of the few owls to take fish out of a lake. Prefers dense deciduous woodlands with sparse undergrowth. Can be attracted with a simple nest box with a large opening, attached to a tree. The young stay with their parents for up to four months after fledging. Often sounds like a dog barking just before giving an eight-hoot call that sounds like, "Who-cooks-for-you? Who-cooks-for-you?" The Great Horned Owl sounds like, "Hoo-hoo-hoo-hoooo!"

male pg. 220

female

YEAR-ROUND

Mallard
Anas platyrhynchos

Size: 20-28" (50-71 cm)

Female: All brown with orange and black bill. Small blue and white wing mark (speculum).

Male: large, bulbous green head, white necklace, rust brown or chestnut chest, combination of gray and white on the sides, yellow bill, orange legs and feet

Juvenile: same as female, but with a yellow bill

Nest: ground; female builds; 1 brood per year

Eggs: 7-10; greenish to whitish, unmarked

Incubation: 26-30 days; female incubates

Fledging: 42-52 days; female leads young to food

Migration: complete, to southern states, non-migrator in Wisconsin

Food: seeds, plants, aquatic insects; will come to ground feeders offering corn

Compare: Female Blue-winged Teal (pg. 140), female Wood Duck (pg. 148) and female Northern Shoveler (pg. 152) are all smaller. Wood Duck has a white eye-ring and Shoveler has a large spoon-shaped bill.

Stan's Notes: A familiar duck of lakes and ponds, it's considered a type of dabbling duck, tipping forward in shallow water to feed on aquatic plants on the bottom. The name "Mallard" comes from the Latin *masculus*, meaning "male," referring to the habit of males not taking part in raising ducklings. Both female and male have white tails and white underwings. Black central tail feathers of male curl upward. Will return to place of birth.

Ring-necked Pheasant
Phasianus colchicus

YEAR-ROUND

Size: 30-36" (76-90 cm), male, including tail
21-25" (53-63 cm), female, including tail

Male: Golden brown body with a long tail. White ring around neck with purple, green, blue and red head.

Female: smaller, less flamboyant all-brown bird with a long tail

Juvenile: similar to female, with a shorter tail

Nest: ground; female builds; 1 brood per year

Eggs: 8-10; olive brown without markings

Incubation: 23-25 days; female incubates

Fledging: 11-12 days; female leads young to food

Migration: non-migrator

Food: insects, seeds, fruit; visits ground feeders

Compare: Ruffed Grouse (pg. 144) is smaller, with a feathered tuft on head, black ruffs on neck and lacks the long pointed tail of female Pheasant. Male Pheasant is brightly colored.

Stan's Notes: Originally introduced to North America from China during the late 1800s. Common now throughout the U.S. Like many other game birds, their numbers vary greatly, making them common in some years and scarce in others. "Ring-necked" refers to the thin white ring around the male's neck. "Pheasant" comes from the Greek word *phaisianos*, meaning "bird of the River Phasis." (The Phasis, located in Europe, is now known as the River Rioni.) Roosts on the ground or in trees at night. Listen for male's cackling call to attract females.

male

soaring

female

soaring

Northern Harrier
Circus cyaneus

YEAR-ROUND
SUMMER

Size: 24" (60 cm); up to 3½-foot wingspan

Male: A slim, low-flying hawk. Silver gray with a large white rump patch and a white belly. Faint narrow bands across the tail. Tips of wings black. Yellow eyes.

Female: dark brown back, a brown-streaked breast and belly, large white rump patch, narrow black bands across tail, tips of wings black, yellow eyes

Juvenile: similar to female, with an orange breast

Nest: platform, often on ground; female and male build; 1 brood per year

Eggs: 4-8; bluish white without markings

Incubation: 31-32 days; female incubates

Fledging: 30-35 days; male and female feed young

Migration: complete, to southern states, Mexico and Central America

Food: mice, snakes, insects, small birds

Compare: Slimmer than Red-tailed Hawk (pg. 162). Look for black tail bands, white rump patch and characteristic flight to help identify.

Stan's Notes: One of the easiest hawks to identify. Harriers glide just above ground, following contours of the land while searching for prey. Holds its wings just above the horizontal position, tilting back and forth in the wind, similar to Turkey Vultures. Formerly called Marsh Hawk due to its habit of hunting over marshes. Feeds on the ground. Will perch on the ground to preen and rest. At any age, has a distinctive owl-like face disk.

soaring

Red-tailed Hawk
Buteo jamaicensis

YEAR-ROUND
SUMMER

Size: 19-25" (48-63 cm); up to 4-foot wingspan

Male: Large hawk with amazing variety of colors from bird to bird, from chocolate brown to nearly all white. Often brown with a white breast and a distinctive brown belly band. Rust red tail, usually seen only from above. Wing underside is white with a small dark patch on leading edge near shoulder.

Female: same as male, only slightly larger

Juvenile: similar to adults, lacking the red tail, has a speckled chest and light eyes

Nest: platform; male and female build; 1 brood per year

Eggs: 2-3; white without markings or sometimes marked with brown

Incubation: 30-35 days; female and male incubate

Fledging: 45-46 days; male and female feed young

Migration: partial migrator to non-migrator

Food: mice, birds, snakes, insects, mammals

Compare: Broad-winged Hawk (pg. 142), Cooper's Hawk (pg. 200) and Sharp-shinned Hawk (pg. 198) are smaller and lack the red tail.

Stan's Notes: A common hawk of open country and in cities, often seen perched on freeway light posts, fences and trees. Look for it circling over open fields and roadsides, searching for prey. Their large stick nests are commonly seen in large trees along roads. Nests are lined with finer material such as evergreen tree needles. Returns to the same nest site each year. Develops red tail in the second year.

Great Horned Owl
Bubo virginianus

YEAR-ROUND

Size: 20-25" (50-63 cm); up to 3½-foot wingspan

Male: Robust brown "horned" owl. Bright yellow eyes and V-shaped white throat resembling a necklace. Horizontal barring on the chest.

Female: same as male, only slightly larger

Juvenile: similar to adults, lacking ear tufts

Nest: no nest; takes over the nests of crows, Great Blue Herons and hawks, or will use partial cavities, stumps or broken-off trees; 1 brood per year

Eggs: 2; white without markings

Incubation: 26-30 days; female incubates

Fledging: 30-35 days; male and female feed young

Migration: non-migrator

Food: mammals, birds (ducks), snakes, insects

Compare: Barred Owl (pg. 154) has dark eyes and no "horns." Over twice the size of its cousin, the Eastern Screech-Owl (pg. 192).

Stan's Notes: One of the earliest nesting birds in the state, laying eggs in January and February. Has excellent hearing; able to hear a mouse moving beneath a foot of snow. "Ears" are actually tufts of feathers (horns) and have nothing to do with hearing. Not able to turn its head all the way around. Wing feathers are ragged on ends, resulting in a silent flight. The eyelids close from the top down, like humans. Fearless, it is one of the few animals that will kill skunks and porcupines. Because of this, it is sometimes called Flying Tiger.

displaying male

non-displaying

female

Wild Turkey
Meleagris gallopavo

YEAR-ROUND

Size: 36-48" (90-120 cm)

Male: Large, plump brown and bronze bird with striking blue and red bare head. Fan tail and long, straight black beard in center of chest. Spurs on legs.

Female: thinner and less striking than male, usually lacking breast beard

Juvenile: same as adult of the same sex

Nest: ground; female builds; 1 brood per year

Eggs: 10-12; buff white with dull brown markings

Incubation: 27-28 days; female incubates

Fledging: 6-10 days; female leads young to food

Migration: non-migrator

Food: insects, seeds, fruit

Compare: This bird is quite distinctive and unlikely to be confused with others.

Stan's Notes: The largest native game bird in Wisconsin, and the bird from which the domestic turkey was bred. Almost became our national bird, losing to the Bald Eagle by a single vote. Eliminated from Wisconsin by the turn of the century due to market hunting and loss of habitat, and reintroduced in the 1950-60s. A strong flier that can approach 60 miles (97 km) per hour. Able to fly straight up, then away. Eyesight is three times better than human eyesight. Hearing is also excellent; can hear competing males up to a mile away. Males hold "harems" of up to 20 females. Males are toms, females are hens and young are poults. Roosts in trees at night.

Ruby-crowned Kinglet
Regulus calendula

MIGRATION
SUMMER

Size: 4" (10 cm)

Male: Small, teardrop-shaped green-to-gray bird with 2 white wing bars and a hidden ruby crown. White eye-ring.

Female: same as male, but lacking the ruby crown

Juvenile: same as female

Nest: pendulous; female builds; 1 brood per year

Eggs: 4-5; white with brown markings

Incubation: 11-12 days; female incubates

Fledging: 11-12 days; female and male feed young

Migration: complete, to southern states, Mexico and Central America

Food: insects, berries

Compare: The female American Goldfinch (pg. 252) is larger, but shares the same olive color and unmarked breast. Look for the white eye-ring of Ruby-crowned Kinglet.

Stan's Notes: This is the second smallest bird in Wisconsin. Most commonly seen during migration in spring and fall, when groups travel together. Look for it flitting around thick shrubs low to the ground. It takes a quick eye to see the male's ruby crown. Female constructs an unusual pendulous (sac-like) nest, intricately woven and decorated on the outside with colored lichens and mosses stuck together with spider webs. The nest is suspended from a branch overlapped by leaves and usually is hung high in a mature tree. The common name "Kinglet" comes from the Anglo-Saxon word *cyning*, or "king," referring to the male's ruby crown, and the diminutive suffix "let," meaning "small."

male

female

Red-breasted Nuthatch
Sitta canadensis

YEAR-ROUND
WINTER

Size: 4½" (11 cm)

Male: A small gray-backed bird with a black cap and a prominent eye line. A rust red breast and belly.

Female: gray cap, pale undersides

Juvenile: same as female

Nest: cavity; female builds; 1 brood per year

Eggs: 5-6; white with red brown markings

Incubation: 11-12 days; female incubates

Fledging: 14-20 days; female and male feed young

Migration: irruptive; moves around the state in search of food

Food: insects, seeds; visits seed and suet feeders

Compare: Smaller than the White-breasted Nuthatch (pg. 178), with a red chest instead of white.

Stan's Notes: The Red-breasted Nuthatch behaves like the White-breasted Nuthatch, climbing down tree trunks headfirst. Similar to chickadees, visits seed feeders, quickly grabbing a seed and flying off to crack it open. Will wedge a seed into a crevice and pound it open with several sharp blows. The name "Nuthatch" comes from the Middle English moniker *nuthak*, referring to the bird's habit of wedging a seed into a crevice and hacking it open. Look for it in mature conifers, where it often extracts seeds from cones. Doesn't excavate a cavity as a chickadee might; rather, it takes over an old woodpecker or chickadee cavity. Common during some winters and scarce in others.

Boreal Chickadee

YEAR-ROUND

Black-capped Chickadee
Poecile atricapillus

Size: 5" (13 cm)

Male: Familiar gray bird with black cap and throat patch. White chest. Tan belly. Small white wing marks.

Female: same as male

Juvenile: same as adult

Nest: cavity; female and male build or excavate; 1 brood per year

Eggs: 5-7; white with fine brown markings

Incubation: 11-13 days; female and male incubate

Fledging: 14-18 days; female and male feed young

Migration: non-migrator

Food: insects, seeds, fruit; comes to seed and suet feeders

Compare: Very similar to Boreal Chickadee (see inset), which has a brown cap and sides. Tufted Titmouse (pg. 180) is larger than the Black-capped Chickadee and has a crest.

Stan's Notes: Backyard bird that is attracted to a nest box or seed feeder. Usually the first to find a new feeder. Can be easily tamed and hand fed. Can be a common urban bird since much of its diet comes from bird feeders. Needs to feed each day in winter; forages for food during even the worst winter storms. Often seen with other birds such as nuthatches and woodpeckers. Builds its nest mostly with green moss and lines it with animal fur. Name comes from its familiar "chika-dee-dee-dee-dee" call. Also gives a high-pitched, two-toned "fee-bee" call. Can have different calls in various regions. Boreal Chickadee is uncommon and found in northern Wisconsin.

male

first winter

female

Yellow-rumped Warbler
Dendroica coronata

MIGRATION
SUMMER

Size: 5-6" (13-15 cm)

Male: Slate gray bird with black streaks on breast. Yellow patches on rump, flanks and head. White chin and belly. Two white wing bars.

Female: duller than male, but same yellow patches

Juvenile: similar to female

Nest: cup; female builds; 2 broods per year

Eggs: 4-5; white with brown markings

Incubation: 12-13 days; female incubates

Fledging: 10-12 days; female and male feed young

Migration: complete, to southern states, Mexico and Central America

Food: insects, berries; rarely comes to suet feeders

Compare: Male Common Yellowthroat (pg. 254) has a yellow breast and very distinctive black mask. Male Yellow Warbler (pg. 256) is all yellow with orange streaks on the breast. Look for patches of yellow on rump, flanks and head of the Yellow-rumped Warbler to help identify.

Stan's Notes: One of our most common warblers, seen in flocks of hundreds during migration. One of the first warblers to return to Wisconsin, arriving in April, and one of the last to leave in autumn. Male molts to a dull color in winter similar to the female, retaining yellow patches. Often called Myrtle Warbler in eastern states and Audubon's Warbler in western states. Sometimes called Butter-butts due to the yellow patch on rump. Builds cup nest in coniferous and aspen forests. Familiar call is a robust "chip."

female
pg. 84

male

Dark-eyed Junco
Junco hyemalis

YEAR-ROUND
WINTER

Size: 5½" (14 cm)

Male: A round, dark-eyed bird with slate gray-to-charcoal chest, head and back. White belly. Pink bill. Since the outermost tail feathers are white, tail appears as a white V in flight.

Female: same as male, only tan-to-brown color

Juvenile: similar to female, but has a streaked breast and head

Nest: cup; female and male construct; 2 broods per year

Eggs: 3-5; white with reddish brown markings

Incubation: 12-13 days; female incubates

Fledging: 10-13 days; male and female feed young

Migration: complete, throughout the U.S.

Food: seeds, insects; will come to seed feeders

Compare: Rarely confused with any other bird. Small flocks feed under bird feeders in winter.

Stan's Notes: One of Wisconsin's most common winter residents. Migrates from Canada to Wisconsin and beyond. The females tend to migrate farther south than the males. Adheres to a rigid social hierarchy, with dominant birds chasing less dominant birds. Look for its white outer tail feathers flashing when in flight. Usually seen in small flocks on the ground, where it will "double-scratch" with both feet simultaneously to expose seeds and insects. Consumes many weed seeds. Nests in a wide variety of wooded habitats. Several junco species have now been combined into one, simply called Dark-eyed Junco.

YEAR-ROUND

White-breasted Nuthatch
Sitta carolinensis

Size: 5-6" (13-15 cm)

Male: Slate gray with a white face and belly, and black cap and nape. Long thin bill, slightly upturned. Chestnut undertail.

Female: similar to male, gray cap and nape

Juvenile: similar to female

Nest: cavity; female and male construct; 1 brood per year

Eggs: 5-7; white with brown markings

Incubation: 11-12 days; female incubates

Fledging: 13-14 days; female and male feed young

Migration: non-migrator

Food: insects, seeds; visits seed and suet feeders

Compare: Red-breasted Nuthatch (pg. 170) is smaller with a rust red belly and a distinctive black eye line.

Stan's Notes: The nuthatch's habit of hopping headfirst down tree trunks helps it see insects and insect eggs that birds climbing up the trunk might miss. Incredible climbing agility comes from an extra-long hind toe claw or nail, nearly twice the size of the front toe claws. The name "Nuthatch" comes from the Middle English moniker *nuthak*, referring to the bird's habit of wedging a seed into a crevice and hacking it open. Often seen in flocks with chickadees, Brown Creepers and Downy Woodpeckers. Mated birds will stay with each other year-round, defending small territories. Listen for its characteristic spring call, "whi-whi-whi-whi," given in February and March. One of 17 worldwide nuthatch species.

Tufted Titmouse
Baeolophus bicolor

YEAR-ROUND

Size: 6" (15 cm)

Male: Slate gray bird with a white chest and belly. Pointed crest. Flanks are washed in a rusty brown. Gray legs and dark eyes.

Female: same as male

Juvenile: same as adult

Nest: cavity; female lines old woodpecker hole; 2 broods per year

Eggs: 5-7; white with brown markings

Incubation: 13-14 days; female incubates

Fledging: 15-18 days; female and male feed young

Migration: non-migrator

Food: insects, seeds, fruit; will come to seed and suet feeders

Compare: Closely related to Black-capped Chickadee (pg. 172), but Titmouse is slightly larger and has a crest. Similar in size and color to the White-breasted Nuthatch (pg. 178), but Nuthatch lacks a crest.

Stan's Notes: A common feeder bird, it can be attracted with black oil sunflower seeds. Well known for its quickly repeated "peter-peter-peter" call. Prefix "Tit" comes from a Scandinavian word meaning "little." Suffix "mouse" is derived from the Old English word *mase*, meaning "bird." Simply translated, it is a "small bird." Notorious for pulling hair from sleeping dogs, cats and squirrels to line their nests. Attracted with nest boxes. Usually seen only one or two at a time. Male feeds female during courtship and nesting.

Eastern Phoebe
Sayornis phoebe

SUMMER

Size: 7" (18 cm)

Male: Gray bird with dark wings, light olive green belly and a thin dark bill.

Female: same as male

Juvenile: same as adult

Nest: cup; female builds; 2 broods per year

Eggs: 4-5; white without markings

Incubation: 15-16 days; female incubates

Fledging: 15-16 days; male and female feed young

Migration: complete, to southern states and Mexico

Food: insects

Compare: Like most other olive gray birds, it is hard to distinguish identifying markings. Eastern Phoebe lacks any white eye-ring. Easier to identify by well-enunciated song, "fee-bee," or characteristic of hawking for insects.

Stan's Notes: A sparrow-sized bird often seen on the end of a dead branch. It sits in wait for a passing insect, flies out to catch it, then returns to the same branch, a process called hawking. Has a habit of pumping its tail up and down and spreading it when perched. Will build its nest under the eaves of a house, under a bridge or in culverts. Nest is constructed with mud, grass and moss, and lined with hair (and sometimes feathers). The name is derived from its characteristic song, "fee-bee," which is repeated over and over from the tops of dead branches.

Eastern Kingbird
Tyrannus tyrannus

SUMMER

Size: 8" (20 cm)

Male: Mostly black gray bird with white belly and chin. Black head and tail with a distinctive white band across the end of the tail. Has a concealed red crown that is rarely seen.

Female: same as male

Juvenile: same as adult

Nest: cup; male and female construct; 1 brood per year

Eggs: 3-4; white with brown markings

Incubation: 16-18 days; female incubates

Fledging: 16-18 days; female and male feed young

Migration: complete, to Mexico, Central America and South America

Food: insects, fruit

Compare: Medium-sized bird, smaller than American Robin (pg. 190). Eastern Phoebe (pg. 182) is smaller and lacks Kingbird's white belly. Look for the white band on Kingbird's tail.

Stan's Notes: A summer resident seen in open fields and prairies. Up to 20 individuals migrate together in a group. Returns to the mating ground in springtime, where male and female defend their territory. Acting unafraid of other birds and chasing the larger ones, it is perceived as having an attitude. Its bold behavior gave rise to the common name, King. Perches on tall branches and watches for insects. After flying out to catch them, returns to the same perch, a technique called hawking. Becomes very vocal during late summer, when entire families call back and forth while hunting for insects.

male pg. 236

female

WINTER

Pine Grosbeak
Pinicola enucleator

Size: 9" (22.5 cm)

Female: A plump gray winter finch with a long dark tail. Dark wings with two white wing bars. Head and rump tinged dull yellow. Short, stubby, pointed dark bill.

Male: overall rosy red and gray

Juvenile: female is similar to adult female, male has a touch of red on head and rump

Nest: cup; female builds; 1 brood per year

Eggs: 4-5; bluish green without markings

Incubation: 13-15 days; female incubates

Fledging: 13-20 days; female and male feed young

Migration: non-migrator to irruptive; moves around to find food

Food: seeds, fruit, insects; will come to feeders

Compare: The female Evening Grosbeak (pg. 264) is slightly smaller and lacks the dull yellow head. Female Crossbill (pg. 258) is smaller, has a long crossed bill and lacks wing bars.

Stan's Notes: A common winter finch in northern Wisconsin in some years and not so common in others. This is a very tame and approachable bird. Often seen along roads or on the ground, eating tiny grains of sand and dirt to aid digestion. A seed eater that favors coniferous woods, rarely moving out of coniferous regions during the summer. Frequently seen bathing in fluffy snow. Flies with a typical finch-like undulating pattern while calling a soft whistle. During breeding season, male and female develop a pouch in the bottom of the mouth (buccal pouch) to transport seeds to young.

SUMMER

Gray Catbird
Dumetella carolinensis

Size: 9" (22.5 cm)

Male: Handsome slate gray bird with black crown and a long, thin black bill. Often seen with its tail lifted up, exposing a chestnut patch under the tail.

Female: same as male

Juvenile: same as adult

Nest: cup; female and male construct; 2 broods per year

Eggs: 4-6; blue green without markings

Incubation: 12-13 days; female incubates

Fledging: 10-11 days; female and male feed young

Migration: complete, to southern states

Food: insects, fruit

Compare: Larger than Eastern Phoebe (pg. 182), it lacks the Phoebe's olive belly. Similar size as Eastern Kingbird (pg. 184), but it lacks the Kingbird's white belly and white tail band.

Stan's Notes: A secretive bird that the Chippewa Indians named Bird That Cries With Grief due to its raspy call. The call sounds like the mewing of a house cat, hence the common name. Frequently mimics other birds, rarely repeating the same phrases. More often heard than seen. Nests in thick shrubs and quickly flies back into shrubs if approached. If a cowbird introduces an egg into a catbird nest, the catbird will quickly break it, then eject it.

American Robin
Turdus migratorius

SUMMER

Size: 9-11" (22.5-28 cm)

Male: A familiar gray bird with a rusty red breast, and nearly black head and tail. White chin with black streaks. White eye-ring.

Female: similar to male, but with a gray head and a duller breast

Juvenile: similar to female, but has a speckled breast and brown back

Nest: cup; female builds with help from the male; 2-3 broods per year

Eggs: 4-7; pale blue without markings

Incubation: 12-14 days; female incubates

Fledging: 14-16 days; female and male feed young

Migration: complete, to southern states, Mexico and Central America; small percentage will not migrate

Food: insects, fruit, berries, earthworms

Compare: Familiar bird to all.

Stan's Notes: Can be heard singing all night long in spring. Most people don't realize how easy it is to differentiate male and female robins. Compare the male's dark, nearly black head and brick red breast with the female's gray head and dull red breast. Robins are not listening for worms when they cock their heads to one side. They are looking with eyes placed far back on the sides of their heads. A very territorial bird. Often seen fighting its own reflection in windows. Small percentage in Wisconsin won't migrate, but will spend the winter in low swampy areas, searching for leftover berries and insect eggs. Some of the non-migrators will die before spring.

red morph

gray morph

Eastern Screech-Owl
Megascops asio

YEAR-ROUND

Size: 9" (22.5 cm); up to 20-inch wingspan

Male: Small "eared" owl that occurs in one of two permanent color morphs. Is either mottled with gray and white or is red brown (rust) with white. Bright yellow eyes.

Female: same as male

Juvenile: lighter color than adult of the same morph, usually no ear tufts

Nest: cavity, former woodpecker cavity; does not add any nesting material; 1 brood per year

Eggs: 4-5; white without markings

Incubation: 25-26 days; female incubates, male feeds female during incubation

Fledging: 26-27 days; male and female feed young

Migration: non-migrator

Food: large insects, small mammals, birds, snakes

Compare: The only small owl in Wisconsin with ear tufts. Can be gray or rust in color.

Stan's Notes: A common owl active at dusk and during the night. Excellent hearing and eyesight. Will seldom give a screeching call; more commonly gives a tremulous, descending whiny trill, like a sound effect of a scary movie. Will nest in a wooden nest box. Often seen sunning themselves at nest box holes during the winter. Male and female may roost together at night, and are thought to mate for life. Different colorations are known as morphs. The gray morph is more common than the red.

Gray Jay
Perisoreus canadensis

YEAR-ROUND

Size: 11½" (29 cm)

Male: A large gray bird with black nape and white chest. Short black bill and dark eyes. White patch on forehead.

Female: same as male

Juvenile: sooty gray with a faint white whisker mark

Nest: cup; male and female construct; 1 brood per year

Eggs: 3-4; gray white, finely marked to unmarked

Incubation: 16-18 days; female incubates

Fledging: 14-15 days; male and female feed young

Migration: non-migrator

Food: insects, seeds, fruit, nuts; visits seed feeders

Compare: Similar size as Blue Jay (pg. 62), but lacks the Blue Jay's crest and blue coloring.

Stan's Notes: A bird of the North Woods. Known as Camp Robber because it rummages through camps looking for food scraps. Also called Whisky Jack or Canada Jay. Easily tamed, this bird will fly to your hand if offered raisins or nuts. Will eat just about anything. Also stores extra food for the winter, balling it together in a sticky mass, placing it on a tree branch, often concealing it with lichen or bark. Travels around in small family units of 3-5, making good companions for campers and canoeists. Reminds some people of an overgrown chickadee.

YEAR-ROUND

Rock Pigeon
Columba livia

Size: 13" (33 cm)

Male: No set color pattern. Gray to white, patches of iridescent greens and blues, usually with a light rump patch.

Female: same as male

Juvenile: same as adult

Nest: platform; female builds; 3-4 broods a year

Eggs: 1-2; white without markings

Incubation: 18-20 days; female and male incubate

Fledging: 25-26 days; female and male feed young

Migration: non-migrator

Food: seeds

Compare: Mourning Dove (pg. 132) is smaller, light brown and lacks all the color variations of the Rock Pigeon.

Stan's Notes: Also known as Domestic Pigeon, formerly known as Rock Dove. Introduced to North America from Europe by the early settlers. This bird is most common around cities and barnyards, where it scratches for seeds. One of the few birds that has a wide variety of colors, produced by years of selective breeding while in captivity. Parents feed their young a regurgitated liquid known as crop-milk for the first few days of life. One of the few birds that can drink without tilting its head back. Nests under bridges and on buildings, balconies, barns and sheds. Was once poisoned as a "nuisance city bird." Many cities now have Peregrine Falcons (not shown) that feed on Rock Pigeons, keeping their numbers in check.

soaring

juvenile

Sharp-shinned Hawk
Accipiter striatus

Size: 10-14" (25-36 cm); up to 2-foot wingspan

Male: Small woodland hawk with a gray back and head and a rusty red breast. Long tail with several dark tail bands, widest band at end of squared-off tail. Red eyes.

Female: same as male, only larger

Juvenile: same size as adults, with a brown back and heavily streaked breast, yellow eyes

Nest: platform; female builds; 1 brood per year

Eggs: 4-5; white with brown markings

Incubation: 32-35 days; female incubates

Fledging: 24-27 days; female and male feed young

Migration: complete, to southern Wisconsin, southern states, Mexico and Central America

Food: birds, small mammals

Compare: Nearly identical to Cooper's Hawk (pg. 200), only smaller. Look for the Sharp-shinned's squared tail compared with the rounded tail of the Cooper's.

Stan's Notes: A common hawk of backyards and woodlands, often seen swooping in on birds visiting feeders. Its short rounded wings and long tail allow this hawk to navigate through thick stands of trees in pursuit of prey. Common name comes from the sharp keel on the leading edge of its "shin," though it is actually below rather than above the bird's ankle on the tarsus bone of foot. The tarsus in most birds is round. In flight, head doesn't protrude as far as the head of the Cooper's Hawk.

 CD 2, TRACK 36

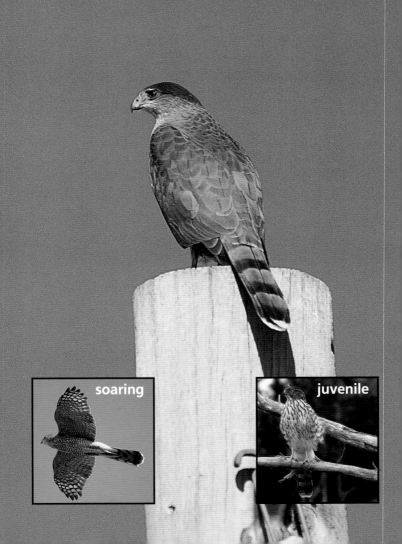

soaring

juvenile

Cooper's Hawk
Accipiter cooperii

YEAR-ROUND
SUMMER

Size: 14-20" (36-50 cm); up to 2½-foot wingspan

Male: Medium-sized hawk with short wings and long rounded tail with several black bands. Rusty breast and dark wing tips. Slate gray back. Bright yellow spot at base of gray bill (cere). Dark red eyes.

Female: similar to male, only slightly larger

Juvenile: brown back with brown streaks on breast, bright yellow eyes

Nest: platform; male and female build; 1 brood per year

Eggs: 2-4; greenish with brown markings

Incubation: 32-36 days; female and male incubate

Fledging: 28-32 days; male and female feed young

Migration: non-migrator to partial migrator; will move around to find food

Food: small birds, mammals

Compare: Nearly identical to the Sharp-shinned Hawk (pg. 198), only larger, darker gray and with a rounded-off tail.

Stan's Notes: A common hawk of woodlands. During flight, look for its large head, short wings and long tail. The stubby wings help it maneuver between trees while pursuing small birds. Comes to feeders, hunting for unaware birds. Flies with long glides followed by a few quick flaps. Known to ambush prey, it will fly into heavy brush or even run on the ground in pursuit. Nestlings have gray eyes that become bright yellow at 1 year of age and dark red later. Can be seen during winter.

winter

in flight

breeding

juvenile

Ring-billed Gull
Larus delawarensis

SUMMER
WINTER

Size: 19" (48 cm); up to 4-foot wingspan

Male: A white bird with gray wings, black wing tips spotted with white, and a white tail, as seen in flight. Yellow bill with a black ring near tip. Yellowish legs and feet. Winter or non-breeding adult has a speckled brown back of head and nape of neck.

Female: same as male

Juvenile: mostly gray version of winter adult, has a dark band at end of tail

Nest: ground; female and male construct; 1 brood per year

Eggs: 2-4; off-white with brown markings

Incubation: 20-21 days; female and male incubate

Fledging: 20-40 days; female and male feed young

Migration: complete, to eastern Wisconsin along Lake Michigan, southern states and Mexico

Food: insects, fish; scavenges for food

Compare: Similar to Herring Gull (pg. 242), which has an orange-red mark on tip of lower bill. Herring Gull has pink legs and feet and lacks a black ring on its bill.

Stan's Notes: A common gull of garbage dumps and parking lots. It is expanding its range and remaining farther north longer during winter due to successful scavenging in cities. A three-year gull with a new, different plumage in each of the first three autumns. Attains ring on bill after its first winter and adult plumage in its third year. Defends a small area around nest.

CD 2, TRACK 38

in flight

Canada Goose
Branta canadensis

YEAR-ROUND
SUMMER

Size: 25-43" (63-109 cm); up to 5½-foot wingspan

Male: Large gray goose with black neck and head, with a white chin or cheek strap.

Female: same as male

Juvenile: same as adult

Nest: platform, on the ground; female builds; 1 brood per year

Eggs: 5-10; white without markings

Incubation: 25-30 days; female incubates

Fledging: 42-55 days; male and female teach young to feed

Migration: non-migrator to partial, to southern states; will move to any place with open water

Food: aquatic plants, insects, seeds

Compare: Large goose that is rarely confused with any other bird.

Stan's Notes: Eliminated from the state in the 1900s. Reintroduced to federal refuges in the 1930s and to local and state lands in the 1960-70s. Once not very common, but has adapted to our changed environment very well. Adults mate for many years, but only start to breed in their third year. Males often act as sentinels, standing at the edge of the group, bobbing their heads up and down, becoming very aggressive to anybody who approaches. Will hiss as if to display displeasure. Adults molt their primary flight feathers while raising young, rendering family groups flightless at the same time. Several subspecies vary geographically across the U.S. Generally it is darker in color in the western groups and paler in eastern. Size decreases northward, with the smallest subspecies found on the Arctic tundra.

in flight

rusty stain

rusty stain
in flight

SUMMER

Sandhill Crane
Grus canadensis

Size: 40-48" (102-120 cm); up to 7-foot wingspan

Male: Elegant gray bird with long legs and neck. Wings and body often stained rusty brown. Scarlet red cap. Yellow-to-red eyes.

Female: same as male

Juvenile: dull brown, lacks red cap, has yellow eyes

Nest: platform, on the ground; female and male build; 1 brood per year

Eggs: 2; olive with brown markings

Incubation: 28-32 days; female and male incubate

Fledging: 65 days; female and male feed young

Migration: complete, to southern states and Mexico

Food: insects, fruit, worms, plants, amphibians

Compare: Similar size as Great Blue Heron (pg. 208), but the Crane has a shorter bill and red cap. Great Blue Heron flies with neck held in an S shape unlike the Crane's straight neck.

Stan's Notes: Among the tallest birds in the world and capable of flying at great heights. Usually seen in large undisturbed fields near water. Has a very distinctive rattling call. Often heard before seen. Plumage often appears rusty brown (see insets) due to staining from mud during preening. A characteristic flight with upstroke quicker than down. Performing a spectacular mating dance, the birds face each other, bow and jump into the air while uttering loud cackling sounds and flapping wings. Often flips sticks and grass into the air during dance.

in flight

SUMMER

Great Blue Heron
Ardea herodias

Size: 42-52" (107-132 cm); up to 6-foot wingspan

Male: Tall gray heron. Black eyebrows extend into several long plumes off the back of head. Long yellow bill. Feathers at base of neck drop down in a kind of necklace.

Female: same as male

Juvenile: same as adult, but more brown than gray, with a black crown and no plumes

Nest: platform; male and female build; 1 brood per year

Eggs: 3-5; blue green without markings

Incubation: 27-28 days; female and male incubate

Fledging: 56-60 days; male and female feed young

Migration: complete, to southern states, Mexico and Central and South America

Food: small fish, frogs, insects, snakes

Compare: Similar size as the Sandhill Crane (pg. 206), but lacks the Crane's red crown. Crane flies with neck held straight unlike the Heron's S-shaped neck.

Stan's Notes: One of the most common herons, often barking like a dog when startled. Seen stalking small fish in shallow water. Will strike at mice, squirrels and just about anything else it might come across. Flies holding neck in an S shape, with its long legs trailing straight out behind. The wings are held in cupped fashion during flight. Nests in colonies of up to 100 birds. Nests in treetops near or over open water.

CD 2, TRACK 41

male

female

SUMMER

Ruby-throated Hummingbird
Archilochus colubris

Size: 3-3½" (7.5-9 cm)

Male: Tiny iridescent green bird with black throat patch that reflects bright ruby red in sun.

Female: same as male, but lacking the throat patch

Juvenile: same as female

Nest: cup; female builds; 1-2 broods per year

Eggs: 2; white without markings

Incubation: 12-14 days; female incubates

Fledging: 14-18 days; female feeds young

Migration: complete, to southern states, Mexico and Central America

Food: nectar, insects; will come to nectar feeders

Compare: No other bird is as tiny. The Sphinx Moth also hovers at flowers, but has clear wings and a mouth part that looks like a straw, which coils up when not at flowers. Doesn't hum in flight, moves much slower than the Hummingbird and can be approached.

Stan's Notes: The smallest bird in Wisconsin. Able to hover, fly up and down, and is the only bird to fly backward. Does not sing, but will chatter or buzz to communicate. The wings create a humming noise, flapping 50-60 times each second or faster during chasing flights. The heart pumps an incredible 1,260 beats per minute, and it breathes 250 times per minute. Weighing just 2-3 grams, it takes about five average-sized hummingbirds to equal the weight of one chickadee. Constructs its nest with plant material and spider webs, gluing pieces of lichen on the outside for camouflage. Attracted to tubular red flowers.

SUMMER

Green Heron
Butorides virescens

Size: 16-22" (40-56 cm)

Male: Short stocky heron with a blue-green back, and rusty red neck and chest. Dark green crest. Short legs, normally yellow, but turn bright orange during breeding season.

Female: same as male

Juvenile: similar to adult, with a blue-gray back and white-streaked chest and neck

Nest: platform; female and male build; 2 broods per year

Eggs: 2-4; light green without markings

Incubation: 21-25 days; female and male incubate

Fledging: 35-36 days; female and male feed young

Migration: complete, to South America

Food: fish, insects, amphibians, aquatic plants

Compare: Much smaller than the Great Blue Heron (pg. 208) and lacks the long neck of most other herons. Look for a small heron with a dark green back stalking wetlands.

Stan's Notes: Often gives an explosive, rasping "skyew" call when startled. Sometimes it looks like it doesn't have a neck, because it holds its head close to its body. Hunts for small fish, aquatic insects and small amphibians by waiting on a shore or wading stealthily. Has been known to place an object such as an insect on the water surface to attract fish to catch. Raises its crest when excited.

female pg. 148

male

Wood Duck
Aix sponsa

SUMMER

Size: 17-20" (43-50 cm)

Male: A small, highly ornamented dabbling duck with a green head and crest patterned with white and black. A rusty chest, white belly and red eyes.

Female: brown, similar size and shape as male, has bright white eye-ring and a not-so-obvious crest, blue patch on wing often hidden

Juvenile: same as female

Nest: cavity; female lines old woodpecker cavity; 1 brood per year

Eggs: 10-15; creamy white without markings

Incubation: 28-36 days; female incubates

Fledging: 56-68 days; female teaches young to feed

Migration: complete, to southern states

Food: aquatic insects, plants, seeds

Compare: Male Northern Shoveler (pg. 216) is larger and has a long wide bill.

Stan's Notes: A common duck of quiet, shallow backwater ponds. Nearly extinct around 1900 due to overhunting, but is doing well now. Nests in an old woodpecker hole or uses a nesting box. Often seen flying deep in forests or perched high on tree branches. Female takes to flight with a loud squealing call and enters nest cavity from full flight. Lays eggs in a neighboring female nest (egg dumping), resulting in some clutches in excess of 20 eggs. Young stay in nest 24 hours after hatching, then jump from up to 30 feet (9 m) to the ground or water to follow their mother, never returning to the nest.

female pg. 152

male

Northern Shoveler
Anas clypeata

MIGRATION
SUMMER

Size: 20" (50 cm)

Male: Medium-sized duck with iridescent green head, rusty sides and white breast. Has an extraordinarily large spoon-shaped bill that is almost always held pointed toward water.

Female: brown and black all over, green speculum, spoon-shaped bill

Juvenile: same as female

Nest: ground; female builds; 1 brood per year

Eggs: 9-12; olive without markings

Incubation: 22-25 days; female incubates

Fledging: 30-60 days; female leads young to food

Migration: complete, to southern states, Mexico and Central America

Food: aquatic insects, plants

Compare: Similar to the male Mallard (pg. 220), but Shoveler has a large, characteristic spoon-shaped bill. Larger than male Wood Duck (pg. 214) and lacks the Wood Duck's crest.

Stan's Notes: One of several species of shoveler, so called because of the peculiar shape of its bill. The Northern Shoveler is the only species of these ducks in North America. Found in small flocks of 5-10, swimming low in water with its large bill pointed toward the water, as if it's too heavy to lift. Feeds mainly by filtering tiny aquatic insects and plants from the water's surface with its bill.

in flight

female pg. 238

male

Common Merganser
Mergus merganser

MIGRATION
SUMMER
WINTER

Size: 27" (69 cm)

Male: Long, thin, duck-like bird with green head, a black back, and white sides, breast and neck. Has a long, pointed orange bill. Often appears to be black and white in poor light.

Female: same size and shape as the male, but with a rust red head, ragged "hair" on head, gray body with white chest and chin, and long, pointed orange bill

Juvenile: same as female

Nest: cavity; female lines old woodpecker cavity; 1 brood per year

Eggs: 9-11; ivory without markings

Incubation: 28-33 days; female incubates

Fledging: 70-80 days; female feeds young

Migration: complete, to southern Wisconsin, southern states, Mexico and Central America

Food: small fish, aquatic insects

Compare: Male Mallard (pg. 220) lacks the black back and long bill. The male Hooded Merganser (pg. 40) has a white patch on the head.

Stan's Notes: The merganser is a shallow water diver that feeds on small fish in 10-15 feet (3-4.5 m) of water. More commonly seen along rivers than lakes. The bill has a fine serrated-like edge to help catch slippery fish. Females often lay eggs in other merganser nests (egg dumping), resulting in broods of up to 15 young per mother. Male leaves the female when she starts to incubate eggs. Orphans are accepted by other merganser mothers with young.

female pg. 156

male

Mallard
Anas platyrhynchos

Size: 27-28" (69-71 cm)

Male: Large, bulbous green head, white necklace and rust brown or chestnut chest. Gray and white on the sides. Yellow bill. Orange legs and feet.

Female: all brown with orange and black bill, small blue and white wing mark (speculum)

Juvenile: same as female, but with a yellow bill

Nest: ground; female builds; 1 brood per year

Eggs: 7-10; greenish to whitish, unmarked

Incubation: 26-30 days; female incubates

Fledging: 42-52 days; female leads young to food

Migration: complete, to southern states, non-migrator in Wisconsin

Food: seeds, plants, aquatic insects; will come to ground feeders offering corn

Compare: Most people recognize this common duck. The male Northern Shoveler (pg. 216) has a white chest with rust on sides and a dark spoon-shaped bill.

Stan's Notes: A familiar duck of lakes and ponds, it's considered a type of dabbling duck, tipping forward in shallow water to feed on aquatic plants on the bottom. The name "Mallard" comes from the Latin *masculus*, meaning "male," referring to the habit of males not taking part in raising ducklings. Black central tail feathers of male curl upward. Both the male and female have white tails and white underwings. Will return to place of birth.

female pg. 250

male

SUMMER

American Redstart
Setophaga ruticilla

Size: 5" (13 cm)

Male: Small, striking black bird with contrasting patches of orange on sides, wings and tail. White belly.

Female: olive brown with yellow patches on sides, wings and tail, white belly

Juvenile: same as female, the juvenile male is tinged orange in the first year

Nest: cup; female builds; 1 brood per year

Eggs: 3-5; off-white with brown markings

Incubation: 12 days; female incubates

Fledging: 9 days; female and male feed young

Migration: complete, to Mexico, Central America and South America

Food: insects, seeds, berries rarely

Compare: Male Red-winged Blackbird (pg. 8) and the male Baltimore Oriole (pg. 224) are much larger at roughly 8 inches (20 cm). The only small black and orange bird flitting around tops of trees.

Stan's Notes: One of the most common and widespread warblers in Wisconsin. Prefers large unbroken tracts of forest. It appears to be hyperactive when feeding, hovering and darting back and forth to glean insects from leaves. Frequently droops its wings and fans tail just before launching out to catch an insect. Look for the male's flashing black and orange colors high up in trees.

 CD 2, TRACK 45

male

female pg. 262

Baltimore Oriole
Icterus galbula

SUMMER

Size: 7-8" (18-20 cm)

Male: Bright flaming orange bird with black head and black extending down nape of neck onto the back. Black wings with white and orange wing bars. An orange tail with black streaks. Gray bill and dark eyes.

Female: pale yellow with orange tones, gray brown wings, white wing bars, gray bill, dark eyes

Juvenile: same as female

Nest: pendulous; female builds; 1 brood per year

Eggs: 4-5; bluish with brown markings

Incubation: 12-14 days; female incubates

Fledging: 12-14 days; female and male feed young

Migration: complete, to Mexico, Central America and South America

Food: insects, fruit, nectar; comes to orange half and nectar feeders

Compare: Male American Redstart (pg. 222) is smaller and has more black than orange.

Stan's Notes: A fantastic songster, this bird is often heard before seen. Easily attracted to a feeder offering grape jelly, orange halves or sugar water (nectar). Parents bring young to feeders. Sits in tops of trees feeding on caterpillars. Female builds a sock-like nest at the outermost branches of tall trees. Often returns to the same area year after year. Some of the last birds to arrive in spring (May) and first to leave in fall (September).

CD 2, TRACK 46

male

female pg. 76

yellow male

YEAR-ROUND

House Finch
Carpodacus mexicanus

Size: 5" (13 cm)

Male: An orange red face, breast and rump, with a brown cap. Brown marking behind eyes. Brown wings streaked with white. A white belly with brown streaks.

Female: brown with a heavily streaked white chest

Juvenile: similar to female

Nest: cup, sometimes in cavities; female builds; 2 broods per year

Eggs: 4-5; pale blue, lightly marked

Incubation: 12-14 days; female incubates

Fledging: 15-19 days; female and male feed young

Migration: non-migrator to partial migrator; will move around to find food

Food: seeds, fruit, leaf buds; will visit seed feeders

Compare: Male Purple Finch (pg. 228) is very similar, but male House Finch lacks the red crown. Look for the streaked breast and belly, and brown cap of male House Finch.

Stan's Notes: Very social bird. Visits feeders in small flocks. Likes nesting in hanging flower baskets. Incubating female is fed by the male. Has a loud, cheerful warbling song. House Finches that were originally introduced to Long Island, New York, from the western U.S. in the 1940s have since populated the entire eastern U.S. Now found throughout the country. Can be the most common bird at your feeders. Suffers from a fatal eye disease that causes the eyes to crust over. Rarely, some males are yellow (see inset) instead of red, probably due to poor diet.

female
pg. 88

male

Purple Finch
Carpodacus purpureus

YEAR-ROUND WINTER

Size: 6" (15 cm)

Male: Raspberry red head, cap, breast, back and rump. Brownish wings and tail.

Female: heavily streaked brown and white bird with large white eyebrows

Juvenile: same as female

Nest: cup; female and male construct; 1 brood per year

Eggs: 4-5; greenish blue with brown markings

Incubation: 12-13 days; female incubates

Fledging: 13-14 days; female and male feed young

Migration: irruptive; moves around the state in search of food

Food: seeds, insects, fruit; comes to seed feeders

Compare: Redder than the orange red of male House Finch (pg. 226), with a clear breast. Male House Finch has a brown cap unlike male Purple Finch's red cap. Male Red Crossbill (pg. 230) has a unique crossed bill.

Stan's Notes: A year-round finch in the northern half of the state and winter resident in the southern half. Its residency in Wisconsin is long-term, unlike the recent invasion of the House Finch. Visits seed feeders along with House Finches, making it hard to tell them apart. Feeds mainly on seeds, with ash tree seeds a very important food source. Prefers open woods or woodland edges. Travels in flocks of up to 50. Has a rich loud song, with a distinctive "tic" note made only during flight. Not a purple color, the Latin species name *purpureus* means "crimson" or other reddish color.

CD 1, TRACK 43

female pg. 258

male

YEAR-ROUND
WINTER

Red Crossbill
Loxia curvirostra

Size: 6½" (16 cm)

Male: Sparrow-sized bird, dirty red to orange with bright red crown and rump. Long, pointed, crossed bill. Dark brown wings and a short dark brown tail.

Female: pale yellow chest, light gray throat patch, a crossed bill, dark brown wings and tail

Juvenile: streaked with tinges of yellow, bill gradually crosses about 2 weeks after fledging

Nest: cup; female builds; 1 brood per year

Eggs: 3-4; bluish white with brown markings

Incubation: 14-18 days; female incubates

Fledging: 16-20 days; female and male feed young

Migration: irruptive; moves around the state in search of food, will wander as far south as Mexico

Food: seeds, leaf buds; comes to seed feeders

Compare: Similar in shape, size and color to the male Purple Finch (pg. 228). Larger than the male House Finch (pg. 226). Look for the unique crossed bill.

Stan's Notes: The long crossed bill is adapted for extracting seeds from pine and spruce cones, its favorite food. Often dangles upside down like a parrot to reach cones. Also seen on the ground where it eats grit, which helps digest food. Plumage can be highly variable among individuals. Nests in coniferous forests. Irruptive behavior makes it more common in some winters and nonexistent in others.

female
pg. 260

male

Scarlet Tanager
Piranga olivacea

MIGRATION
SUMMER

Size: 7" (18 cm)

Male: Bright scarlet red bird with jet black wings and tail. Ivory bill and dark eyes.

Female: drab greenish yellow bird with olive wings and tail, whitish wing linings, dark eyes

Juvenile: same as female

Nest: cup; female builds; 1 brood per year

Eggs: 4-5; blue green with brown markings

Incubation: 13-14 days; female incubates

Fledging: 9-11 days; female and male feed young

Migration: complete, to Central and South America

Food: insects, fruit

Compare: Male Northern Cardinal (pg. 234) has a black mask and red bill and lacks the black wings of male Scarlet Tanager.

Stan's Notes: This is a tropical-looking bird that prefers mature, unbroken woodlands, where it hunts for insects high in the tops of trees. Requires at least 4 acres (1.5 ha) for nesting; prefers 8 acres (3 ha). It arrives late in spring and leaves early in fall. Male sheds (molts) its bright red plumage in the fall, appearing more like the female. Scarlet Tanagers are included in some 240 tanager species in the world. Nearly all are brightly colored and live in the tropics. The common name "Tanager" comes from a South American Tupi Indian word meaning "any small, brightly colored bird."

female pg. 114

male

juvenile

YEAR-ROUND

Northern Cardinal
Cardinalis cardinalis

Size: 8-9" (20-22.5 cm)

Male: All-red bird with a black mask that extends from the face down to the chin and throat. Large red bill and crest.

Female: buff brown with tinges of red on crest and wings, same black mask and red bill

Juvenile: same as female, but with a blackish gray bill

Nest: cup; female builds; 2-3 broods per year

Eggs: 3-4; bluish white with brown markings

Incubation: 12-13 days; female and male incubate

Fledging: 9-10 days; female and male feed young

Migration: non-migrator

Food: seeds, insects, fruit; comes to seed feeders

Compare: The male Red Crossbill (pg. 230) has dark brown wings and a thinner crossed bill. The male Scarlet Tanager (pg. 232) has black wings and tail. Look for Northern Cardinal's black mask, large crest and red bill.

Stan's Notes: A familiar backyard bird. Look for the male feeding female during courtship. Male feeds young of the first brood by himself while female builds second nest. The name comes from the Latin word *cardinalis*, which means "important." Very territorial in spring, it will fight its own reflection in a window. Non-territorial during winter, gathering in small flocks of up to 20 birds. Both the male and female sing and can be heard anytime of year. Listen for its "whata-cheer-cheer-cheer" territorial call in the spring.

CD 1, TRACK 53

male

female pg. 186

Pine Grosbeak
Pinicola enucleator

WINTER

Size: 9" (22.5 cm)

Male: Plump rosy red and gray winter finch with long dark tail. Dark wings have smattering of gray and two white wing bars. A short, stubby, pointed dark bill.

Female: mostly gray with dark wings and tail, head and rump tinged dull yellow

Juvenile: male has a touch of red on head and rump, female is similar to adult female

Nest: cup; female builds; 1 brood per year

Eggs: 4-5; bluish green without markings

Incubation: 13-15 days; female incubates

Fledging: 13-20 days; female and male feed young

Migration: non-migrator to irruptive; moves around to find food

Food: seeds, fruit, insects; will come to feeders

Compare: Male Red Crossbill (pg. 230) has a crossed bill. Much larger than male Purple Finch (pg. 228) and male House Finch (pg. 226).

Stan's Notes: A common winter finch in northern Wisconsin in some years and not so common in others. This is a very tame and approachable bird. Often seen along roads or on the ground, eating tiny grains of sand and dirt to aid digestion. A seed eater that favors coniferous woods, rarely moving out of coniferous regions during the summer. Frequently seen bathing in fluffy snow. Flies with a typical finch-like undulating pattern while calling a soft whistle. During breeding season, male and female develop a pouch in the bottom of the mouth (buccal pouch) to transport seeds to young.

in flight

male pg. 218

female

Common Merganser
Mergus merganser

MIGRATION
SUMMER
WINTER

Size: 27" (69 cm)

Female: A long, thin, duck-like bird with a rust red head and ragged "hair" on the back of head. Gray body with white chest and chin. Long, pointed orange bill.

Male: same size and shape as the female, but with a green head, black back, white sides and chest, and long, pointed orange bill

Juvenile: same as female

Nest: cavity; female lines old woodpecker cavity; 1 brood per year

Eggs: 9-11; ivory without markings

Incubation: 28-33 days; female incubates

Fledging: 70-80 days; female feeds young

Migration: complete, to southern Wisconsin, southern states, Mexico and Central America

Food: small fish, aquatic insects

Compare: Female Hooded Merganser (pg. 146) has a similar shape, but is much smaller. Look for ragged "hair" on head, a long, pointed orange bill and white chest and chin.

Stan's Notes: The merganser is a shallow water diver that feeds on small fish in 10-15 feet (3-4.5 m) of water. More commonly seen along rivers than lakes. The bill has a fine serrated-like edge to help catch slippery fish. Females often lay eggs in other merganser nests (egg dumping), resulting in broods of up to 15 young per mother. Male leaves the female when she starts to incubate eggs. Orphans are accepted by other merganser mothers with young.

CD 2, TRACK 44

in flight

Common Tern
Sterna hirundo

Size: 13-16" (33-40 cm)

Male: White and gray tern with a jet black crown. Red-orange bill with a black tip. Long white forked "tern" tail. Feet and legs red. Tips of wings dark gray when seen in flight.

Female: same as male

Juvenile: similar to adult, with a blue-gray back and white-streaked chest and neck, incomplete brown-to-black crown

Nest: ground; female and male construct; 1 brood per year

Eggs: 1-3; olive brown with brown markings

Incubation: 21-27 days; female and male incubate

Fledging: 26-27 days; female and male feed young

Migration: complete, to South America

Food: fish, aquatic insects

Compare: Similar to other terns. Look for the jet black crown and red-orange bill with a black tip.

Stan's Notes: This tern was nearly eliminated from the state prior to 1900 due to plume hunting. Protected by 1910, it has made a comeback. Catches small fish by diving into water headfirst. Will catch insects in flight. Arrives during April at nesting grounds. Nest is often in sand or pebbles and lined with grass, shells and aquatic plants. Nests in small colonies. Competition and predation from gulls and birds of prey keep the population from expanding.

breeding

winter

juvenile

YEAR-ROUND
MIGRATION
SUMMER

Herring Gull
Larus argentatus

Size: 23-26" (58-66 cm); up to 5-foot wingspan

Male: Snow-white bird with slate gray wings and black wing tips with tiny white spots. Bill is yellow with an orange-red spot near tip of the lower bill. Pinkish legs. Winter plumage head and neck are dirty gray to brown.

Female: same as male

Juvenile: uniformly mottled brown to gray, black bill

Nest: ground; female and male construct; 1 brood per year

Eggs: 2-3; olive with brown markings

Incubation: 24-28 days; female and male incubate

Fledging: 35-36 days; female and male feed young

Migration: complete, to southern states, non-migrator along the Great Lakes coasts

Food: fish, insects, clams, eggs, baby birds

Compare: Larger than the Ring-billed Gull (pg. 202), which has yellowish legs, a black ring near the tip of its bill and lacks the orange-red spot on its lower mandible.

Stan's Notes: Common gull of large lakes. An opportunistic bird, scavenging for food from dumpsters, but will also take other birds' eggs and young right from nest. Often drops clams and other shellfish from heights to break shells and get to the soft interior. Nests in colonies, returning to same site year after year. Lines ground nest with grasses and seaweed. Takes about four years for juveniles to obtain adult plumage. Adults molt to a dirty gray in the winter, and look similar to juveniles.

 CD 2, TRACK 50

white
morph

blue morph

juvenile

in flight

Snow Goose
Chen caerulescens

Size: 25-38" (63-96 cm); up to 4½-foot wingspan

Male: A mostly white goose with varying patches of black and brown. Black wing tips. Pink bill and legs. Some birds are grayish with a white head.

Female: same as male

Juvenile: overall dull gray with a dark bill

Nest: ground; female builds; 1 brood per year

Eggs: 3-5; white without markings

Incubation: 23-25 days; female incubates

Fledging: 45-49 days; female and male teach young to feed

Migration: complete, to southern states and Mexico

Food: aquatic insects and plants

Compare: Tundra Swan (pg. 248) is much larger and lacks the black wing tips. Smaller than the Canada Goose (pg. 204), which has a black neck and white chin strap.

Stan's Notes: Two color morphs. The more common white morph is pure white with black wing tips. The gray morph is frequently called blue, with a white head, gray breast and back, and pink bill and legs. Has a thick, serrated bill for pulling up plants. Breeds in large colonies on the tundra of northern Canada. Females do not breed until they reach 2-3 years of age. Older females produce more eggs and are more successful than the younger females. Seen by the thousands during migration.

in flight

SUMMER

Great Egret
Ardea alba

Size: 38" (96 cm); up to 4½-foot wingspan

Male: Tall, thin, elegant all-white bird with long, pointed yellow bill. Black stilt-like legs and black feet.

Female: same as male

Juvenile: same as adult

Nest: platform; male and female build; 1 brood per year

Eggs: 2-3; light blue without markings

Incubation: 23-26 days; female and male incubate

Fledging: 43-49 days; female and male feed young

Migration: complete, to southern states, Mexico and Central America

Food: fish, aquatic insects, frogs, crayfish

Compare: Great Blue Heron (pg. 208) has a similar shape, but is larger in size and is not white.

Stan's Notes: A tall and stately bird, the Great Egret slowly stalks shallow wetlands looking for small fish to spear with its long sharp bill. Nests in colonies of up to 100 individuals. Now protected, it was hunted to near extinction in the 1800s and early 1900s for its long white plumage. The common name "Egret" came from the French word *aigrette*, which means "ornamental tufts of plumes." The plumes grow near the tail during breeding season.

juvenile

in flight

MIGRATION

Tundra Swan
Cygnus columbianus

Size: 50-54" (127-137 cm); up to 5½-ft. wingspan

Male: Large all-white swan. A black bill, legs and feet. Small yellow mark in front of each eye.

Female: same as male

Juvenile: same size as adult, gray plumage, pinkish gray bill

Nest: ground; female and male construct; 1 brood per year

Eggs: 4-5; creamy white without markings

Incubation: 35-40 days; female and male incubate

Fledging: 60-70 days; female and male feed young

Migration: complete, to the East coast

Food: plants, aquatic insects

Compare: Snow Goose (pg. 244) is much smaller and has black wing tips. Look for Swan's black bill and legs.

Stan's Notes: Nests on the tundra of northern Canada and Alaska, hence its common name. Migrates diagonally across North America to reach wintering grounds on the East coast. Flies in large V-shaped wedges. Gathers in large numbers in some lakes and rivers to rest for a day or two, then continues migration. Frequently seen in large family groups of 20 or more individuals. Usually seen only during migration. Gives a high-pitched, whistle-like call. Young are easy to distinguish by their gray plumage and pinkish bills.

male pg. 222

female

American Redstart
Setophaga ruticilla

SUMMER

Size: 5" (13 cm)

Female: Olive brown with yellow patches on sides, wings and tail. White belly.

Male: small, striking black bird with contrasting patches of orange on sides, wings and tail, white belly

Juvenile: same as female, the juvenile male is tinged orange in the first year

Nest: cup; female builds; 1 brood per year

Eggs: 3-5; off-white with brown markings

Incubation: 12 days; female incubates

Fledging: 9 days; female and male feed young

Migration: complete, to Mexico, Central America and South America

Food: insects, seeds, berries rarely

Compare: Similar to female Yellow-rumped Warbler (pg. 174), but lacks Warbler's yellow patch on rump.

Stan's Notes: One of the most common and widespread warblers in Wisconsin. Prefers large unbroken tracts of forest. It appears to be hyperactive when feeding, hovering and darting back and forth to glean insects from leaves. Frequently droops its wings and fans tail just before launching out to catch an insect. Look for the male's flashing black and orange colors high up in trees.

winter male

male

female

American Goldfinch

Carduelis tristis

Size: 5" (13 cm)

Male: A perky yellow bird with a black patch on forehead. Black tail with conspicuous white rump. Black wings with white wing bars. No marking on the chest. Dramatic change in color during winter, similar to female.

Female: dull olive yellow without a black forehead, with brown wings and a white rump

Juvenile: same as female

Nest: cup; female builds; 1 brood per year

Eggs: 4-6; pale blue without markings

Incubation: 10-12 days; female incubates

Fledging: 11-17 days; female and male feed young

Migration: partial; flocks of up to 20 individuals move around North America

Food: seeds, insects; will come to seed feeders

Compare: The male Yellow Warbler (pg. 256) is yellow with orange streaks on the chest. Pine Siskin (pg. 80) has a streaked chest and belly, and yellow wing bars. Both female House Finch (pg. 76) and Purple Finch (pg. 88) have heavily streaked chests.

Stan's Notes: Most often found in open fields, scrubby areas and woodlands. Often called Wild Canary. A feeder bird that enjoys Nyjer thistle. Late summer nesting, uses the silky down from wild thistle for nest. Appears roller-coaster-like in flight. Listen for it to twitter during flight. Almost always in small flocks. Moves only far enough south to find food.

YEAR-ROUND

male

female

SUMMER

Common Yellowthroat
Geothlypis trichas

Size: 5" (13 cm)

Male: Olive brown bird with bright yellow throat and breast, a white belly and a distinctive black mask outlined in white. A long, thin, pointed black bill.

Female: similar to male, lacks the black mask

Juvenile: same as female

Nest: cup; female builds; 2 broods per year

Eggs: 3-5; white with brown markings

Incubation: 11-12 days; female incubates

Fledging: 10-11 days; female and male feed young

Migration: complete, to southern states, Mexico and Central America

Food: insects

Compare: Found in a similar habitat as the American Goldfinch (pg. 252), but lacks the male's black forehead and wings. The male Yellow Warbler (pg. 256) has fine orange streaks on the breast and lacks male Yellowthroat's mask. Yellow-rumped Warbler (pg. 174) has only spots of yellow compared with the Yellowthroat's bright yellow breast.

Stan's Notes: A common warbler of open fields and marshes. Has a cheerful, well-known song, "witchity-witchity-witchity-witchity." The male performs a curious courtship display, bouncing in and out of tall grass while uttering an unusual song. The young remain dependent upon the parents longer than most warblers. A frequent cowbird host.

Yellow Warbler
Dendroica petechia

Size: 5" (13 cm)

Male: Yellow warbler with orange streaks on the chest and belly. Long, pointed dark bill.

Female: same as male, but lacking orange streaking

Juvenile: similar to female, only much duller

Nest: cup; female builds; 1 brood per year

Eggs: 4-5; white with brown markings

Incubation: 11-12 days; female incubates

Fledging: 10-12 days; female and male feed young

Migration: complete, to southern states, Mexico and Central and South America

Food: insects

Compare: Yellow-rumped Warbler (pg. 174) has only spots of yellow unlike the orange streaking on the chest of male Yellow Warbler. Male American Goldfinch (pg. 252) has a black forehead and wings. The female Warbler is similar to the female American Goldfinch (pg. 252), but lacks white wing bars.

Stan's Notes: A widespread, common summer warbler in the state, seen in gardens and shrubby areas near water. It is a prolific insect eater, gleaning small caterpillars and other insects from tree leaves. Male is often seen higher up in trees than the female. Female is less conspicuous. Starts to migrate south in July and is gone by August. Males arrive 1-2 weeks before females to claim territories. Migrates at night in mixed flocks of warblers. Rests and feeds during the day.

female

male pg. 230

Red Crossbill
Loxia curvirostra

YEAR-ROUND
WINTER

Size: 6½" (16 cm)

Female: A pale yellow-gray sparrow-sized bird with a pale yellow chest and light gray patch on the throat. Long, pointed, crossed bill. Dark brown wings and a short dark brown tail.

Male: dirty red to orange with a bright red crown and rump, a crossed bill, dark brown wings and a short dark brown tail

Juvenile: streaked with tinges of yellow, bill gradually crosses about 2 weeks after fledging

Nest: cup; female builds; 1 brood per year

Eggs: 3-4; bluish white with brown markings

Incubation: 14-18 days; female incubates

Fledging: 16-20 days; female and male feed young

Migration: irruptive; moves around the state in search of food, will wander as far south as Mexico

Food: seeds, leaf buds; comes to seed feeders

Compare: Larger than the female American Goldfinch (pg. 252). Shape and size are similar to the female Purple Finch (pg. 88). Look for the unique crossed bill.

Stan's Notes: The long crossed bill is adapted for extracting seeds from pine and spruce cones, its favorite food. Often dangles upside down like a parrot to reach cones. Also seen on the ground where it eats grit, which helps digest food. Plumage can be highly variable among individuals. Nests in coniferous forests. Irruptive behavior makes it more common in some winters and nonexistent in others.

female

male pg. 232

Scarlet Tanager
Piranga olivacea

MIGRATION
SUMMER

Size: 7" (18 cm)

Female: Drab greenish yellow bird with olive wings and tail. Whitish wing linings. Dark eyes.

Male: bright scarlet red bird with jet black wings and tail, ivory bill and dark eyes

Juvenile: same as female

Nest: cup; female builds; 1 brood per year

Eggs: 4-5; blue green with brown markings

Incubation: 13-14 days; female incubates

Fledging: 9-11 days; female and male feed young

Migration: complete, to Central and South America

Food: insects, fruit

Compare: The female Baltimore Oriole (pg. 262) has gray brown wings and white wing bars. Female American Goldfinch (pg. 252) is smaller and has white wing bars.

Stan's Notes: This is a tropical-looking bird that prefers mature, unbroken woodlands, where it hunts for insects high in the tops of trees. Requires at least 4 acres (1.5 ha) for nesting; prefers 8 acres (3 ha). It arrives late in spring and leaves early in fall. Male sheds (molts) its bright red plumage in the fall, appearing more like the female. Scarlet Tanagers are included in some 240 tanager species in the world. Nearly all are brightly colored and live in the tropics. The common name "Tanager" comes from a South American Tupi Indian word meaning "any small, brightly colored bird."

male pg. 224

female

Baltimore Oriole
Icterus galbula

SUMMER

Size: 7-8" (18-20 cm)

Female: A pale yellow bird with orange tones, gray brown wings, white wing bars, a gray bill and dark eyes.

Male: bright flaming orange bird with black head and black extending down nape of neck onto the back, black wings with white and orange wing bars, an orange tail with black streaks, gray bill and dark eyes

Juvenile: same as female

Nest: pendulous; female builds; 1 brood per year

Eggs: 4-5; bluish with brown markings

Incubation: 12-14 days; female incubates

Fledging: 12-14 days; female and male feed young

Migration: complete, to Mexico, Central America and South America

Food: insects, fruit, nectar; comes to orange half and nectar feeders

Compare: Female Baltimore Oriole is often confused with the female Scarlet Tanager (pg. 260), which has olive-colored wings.

Stan's Notes: A fantastic songster, this bird is often heard before seen. Easily attracted to a feeder offering grape jelly, orange halves or sugar water (nectar). Parents bring young to feeders. Sits in tops of trees feeding on caterpillars. Female builds a sock-like nest at the outermost branches of tall trees. Often returns to the same area year after year. Some of the last birds to arrive in spring (May) and first to leave in fall (September).

CD 2, TRACK 46

male

juvenile

female

Evening Grosbeak
Coccothraustes vespertinus

YEAR-ROUND
WINTER

Size: 8" (20 cm)

Male: A striking bird with a stocky body, a large ivory-to-greenish bill and bright yellow eyebrows. Dirty yellow head, yellow rump and belly and black-and-white wings and tail.

Female: similar to male, with softer colors and a gray head and throat

Juvenile: similar to female, with a brown bill

Nest: cup; female builds; 1 brood per year

Eggs: 3-4; blue with brown markings

Incubation: 12-14 days; female incubates

Fledging: 13-14 days; female and male feed young

Migration: irruptive; moves around the state in search of food

Food: seeds, insects, fruit; comes to seed feeders

Compare: Larger than its close relative, the Goldfinch (pg. 252). The female Evening Grosbeak is slightly smaller than female Pine Grosbeak (pg. 186) and has a gray head. Look for the male Evening Grosbeak's dark head, bright yellow eyebrows and large thick bill.

Stan's Notes: One of the largest finches. Characteristic undulating finch-like flight. An unusually large bill for cracking seeds, its main food source. Often seen on gravel roads eating gravel, from which it gets minerals, salt and grit to grind the seeds it eats. Sheds the outer layer of its bill in spring, exposing a blue green bill. Moves in large flocks in winter, searching for food, often coming to feeders. More numerous in some years than others.

Eastern Meadowlark
Sturnella magna

SUMMER

Size: 9" (22.5 cm)

Male: Robin-shaped bird with a yellow breast and belly, brown back and a prominent black V-shaped necklace. White outer tail feathers.

Female: same as male

Juvenile: same as adult

Nest: cup, on the ground in dense cover; female builds; 2 broods per year

Eggs: 3-5; white with brown markings

Incubation: 13-15 days; female incubates

Fledging: 11-12 days; female and male feed young

Migration: complete, to southern states, Mexico and Central America

Food: insects, seeds

Compare: Horned Lark (pg. 108) is smaller and lacks a yellow breast and belly. Look for a distinct black V mark on Meadowlark's breast.

Stan's Notes: A bird of open grassy country. Named "Meadowlark" because it's a bird of meadows and sings like the larks of Europe. Best known for its wonderful song—a flute-like, clear whistle. Often seen perching on fence posts, it will quickly dive into tall grass if approached. Conspicuous white markings on each side of its tail, most often seen when flying away. Nest is sometimes domed with dried grass. Not a member of the lark family, it actually belongs to the blackbird family and is related to grackles and orioles. Ranges of Eastern and Western Meadowlarks overlap in the state (map reflects the combined range). The birds are hard to distinguish, but Western is paler yellow and grayer than Eastern and sings a different song.

HELPFUL RESOURCES

Birder's Bug Book, The. Waldbauer, Gilbert. Cambridge: Harvard University Press, 1998.

Birder's Dictionary. Cox, Randall T. Helena, MT: Falcon Press Publishing, 1996.

Birder's Handbook, The. Ehrlich, Paul R., David S. Dobkin and Darryl Wheye. New York: Simon and Schuster, 1988.

Birds Do It, Too: The Amazing Sex Life of Birds. Harrison, Kit and George H. Harrison. Minocqua, WI: Willow Creek Press, 1997.

Birds of Forest, Yard, and Thicket. Eastman, John. Mechanicsburg, PA: Stackpole Books, 1997.

Birds of North America. Kaufman, Kenn. New York: Houghton Mifflin, 2000.

Blackbirds of the Americas. Orians, Gordon H. Seattle: University of Washington Press, 1985.

Cardinal, The. Osborne, June. Austin: University of Texas Press, 1995.

Cry of the Sandhill Crane, The. Grooms, Steve. Minocqua, WI: NorthWord Press, 1992.

Dictionary of American Bird Names, The. Choate, Ernest A. Boston: Harvard Common Press, 1985.

Everything You Never Learned About Birds. Rupp, Rebecca. Pownal, VT: Storey Publishing, 1997.

Field Guide to the Birds, A: A Completely New Guide to All the Birds of Eastern and Central North America. Peterson, Roger Tory and Virginia Marie Peterson. Boston: Houghton Mifflin, 1998.

Field Guide to the Birds of North America: Third Edition. Washington, DC: National Geographic Society, 1999.

Field Guide to Warblers of North America, A. Dunn, Jon and Kimball Garrett. Boston: Houghton Mifflin, 1997.

Folklore of Birds. Martin, Laura C. Old Saybrook, CT: Globe Pequot Press, 1996.

Guide to Bird Behavior, A: Vol I, II, III. Stokes, Donald and Lillian Stokes. Boston: Little, Brown and Company, 1989.

How Birds Migrate. Kerlinger, Paul. Mechanicsburg, PA: Stackpole Books, 1995.

Lives of Birds, The: Birds of the World and Their Behavior. Short, Lester L. Collingdale, PA: DIANE Publishing, 2000.

Living on the Wind. Weidensaul, Scott. New York: North Point Press, 2000.

National Audubon Society: North American Birdfeeder Handbook. Burton, Robert. New York: Dorling Kindersley Publishing, 1995.

National Audubon Society: The Sibley Guide to Bird Life and Behavior. Edited by David Allen Sibley, Chris Elphick and John B. Dunning, Jr. New York: Alfred A. Knopf, 2001.

National Audubon Society: The Sibley Guide to Birds. Sibley, David Allen. New York: Alfred A. Knopf, 2000.

Photographic Guide to North American Raptors, A. Wheeler, Brian K. and William S. Clark. New York: Academic Press, 1999.

Raptors of Eastern North America: The Wheeler Guides. Wheeler, Brian K. Princeton, NJ: Princeton University Press, 2003.

Secret Lives of Birds, The. Gingras, Pierre. Toronto: Key Porter Books, 1997.

Secrets of the Nest. Dunning, Joan. Boston: Houghton Mifflin, 1994.

Sparrows and Buntings: A Guide to the Sparrows and Buntings of North America and the World. Byers, Clive, Jon Curson and Urban Olsson. New York: Houghton Mifflin, 1995.

Stokes Bluebird Book: The Complete Guide to Attracting Bluebirds. Stokes, Donald and Lillian Stokes. Boston: Little, Brown and Company, 1991.

Stokes Field Guide to Birds: Eastern Region. Stokes, Donald and Lillian Stokes. Boston: Little, Brown and Company, 1996.

Stokes Purple Martin Book. Stokes, Donald and Lillian Stokes. Boston: Little, Brown and Company, 1997.

Wisconsin Birdlife: Population and Distribution Past and Present. Robbins, Samuel D., Jr. Madison: University of Wisconsin Press, 1991.

Wisconsin Birds: A Seasonal and Geographical Guide, Second Edition. Temple, Stanley A., John R. Cary and Robert Rolley. Madison: University of Wisconsin Press, 1997.

Wisconsin Birding Hotlines

To report unusual bird sightings or possibly hear recordings of where birds have been seen, you can often call pre-recorded hotlines detailing such information. Since these hotlines are usually staffed by volunteers, and phone numbers and even the organizations that host them often change, the phone numbers are not listed here. To obtain the numbers, go to your favorite internet search engine, type in something like "rare bird alert hotline Wisconsin" and follow the links provided.

Web Pages

The internet is a valuable place to learn more about birds. You may find birding on the net a fun way to discover additional information or to spend a long winter night. These websites will assist you in your pursuit of birds. If a web address doesn't work (they often change a bit), just enter the name of the group into a search engine to track down the new web address.

Site	Address
Wisconsin Society for Ornithology	www.wsobirds.org
Birds of the Great Lakes Region	www.great-lakes.net/envt/flora-fauna/wildlife/bird
American Birding Association	www.aba.org
Cornell Lab of Ornithology	www.birds.cornell.edu
Author Stan Tekiela's home page	www.naturesmart.com

CHECKLIST/INDEX BY SPECIES

Use the boxes to check the birds you've seen.

"CD Track" refers to the *Birds of Wisconsin Audio CDs* by Stan Tekiela.

270

"CD Track" refers to the *Birds of Wisconsin Audio CDs* by Stan Tekiela.

Bird	Page(s)	CD	Track

"CD Track" refers to the *Birds of Wisconsin Audio CDs* by Stan Tekiela.

"CD Track" refers to the *Birds of Wisconsin Audio CDs* by Stan Tekiela.

ABOUT THE AUTHOR

Naturalist, wildlife photographer and writer Stan Tekiela is the originator of the popular state-specific field guide series that includes *Mammals of Wisconsin Field Guide*. For about three decades, Stan has authored more than 120 field guides, nature appreciation books and wildlife audio CDs for nearly every state in the nation, presenting many species of birds, mammals, reptiles and amphibians, trees, wildflowers and cacti. Holding a Bachelor of Science degree in Natural History from the University of Minnesota and as an active professional naturalist for more than 25 years, Stan studies and photographs wildlife throughout the United States and has received various national and regional awards for his books and photographs. Also a well-known columnist and radio personality, his syndicated column appears in more than 20 newspapers and his wildlife programs are broadcast on a number of Midwest radio stations. Stan can be followed on Facebook and also Twitter. He can be contacted via his web page at www.naturesmart.com.